The
BONSAI
Bible

The BONSAI Bible

Peter Chan

The definitive guide to choosing and growing bonsai

MITCHELL BEAZLEY

Dedication

This book is dedicated to my soul mate Dawn, who has been a constant source of inspiration throughout my bonsai journey.

An Hachette UK Company
www.hachette.co.uk

First published in Great Britain in 2014 by Hamlyn, a division of Octopus Publishing Group Ltd, Endeavour House, 189 Shaftesbury Avenue, London WC2H 8JY
www.octopusbooks.co.uk

Distributed in the US by Hachette Book Group USA, 237 Park Avenue, New York, NY 10017, USA

Distributed in Canada by Canadian Manda Group, 165 Dufferin Street, Toronto, Ontario, Canada M6K 3H6

Some of the material in this book was originally published in *Choosing and Growing Bonsai* by Peter Chan (2007).

Peter Chan asserts the moral right to be identified as the author of this work.

ISBN 978-1-84533-908-1

A CIP catalogue record for this book is available from the British Library.

Printed and bound in China.

10 9 8 7 6 5 4 3 2 1

Contents

Introduction	6
All about bonsai	8
Looking after bonsai	26
Outdoor coniferous bonsai	42
Outdoor broad-leaved bonsai	104
Outdoor flowering bonsai	170
Indoor/tropical and subtropical bonsai	238
Index	314
Acknowledgements	320

Introduction

Bonsai are now part of our lives. Like oriental food, they are now taken for granted and most people are familiar with them. No longer are these tiny trees regarded as curiosities or botanical freaks, as they were a few decades ago. There was a time when they were available only at specialist centres, but now it is possible to buy bonsai in shopping malls and on the internet. These plants can also be found at garden centres and horticultural shows.

Some bonsai are relatively inexpensive, while others can be very costly. As with any commodity, the different styles and grades of bonsai are reflected in the price. You can buy a young, newly trained bonsai with very limited funds, or you can spend thousands on an exquisite masterpiece that has been shown at major exhibitions in Japan. Serious enthusiasts regard good-quality bonsai as works of art, and these are highly collectable items.

Although the art of bonsai is essentially about growing trees, for many people it is much more than that. Bonsai plants convey something about the owner's lifestyle, aesthetic sense and attitude towards nature and the environment. Growing bonsai has come to be associated with Zen aesthetics, and some practitioners derive a special therapeutic benefit, which comes from the innate peace and tranquility that working with bonsai imparts. Like yoga

Left: Common juniper is ideal for training in the driftwood style.

and t'ai chi, bonsai are said to have a calming influence on the mind and spirit, and they can help to relieve the stresses of today's busy world.

Bonsai are certainly beautiful to look at, but there is much more to the pastime than simply achieving beauty. The image of an ancient tree clinging to a rock and struggling to survive against all the odds has been a source of inspiration for Chinese sages and scholars for at least two millennia.

Keeping bonsai is not just about gardening – it is art and spirituality combined with horticultural techniques. Creating bonsai is a challenge, and enthusiasts are forever striving for

horticultural and aesthetic excellence. Unlike other artistic projects, however, a bonsai is never finished. It continues to grow and change, which means that perfection is always transitory and beauty is only momentary. Growing bonsai is a never-ending quest for perfection.

Those who are dedicated to the hobby regard it as a way of life. It requires commitment and can dictate the way you spend your time and resources. Your weekends and holidays can soon become geared around your bonsai activities. Nevertheless, the rewards that come from striving for a perfect work of art more than compensate for the time and effort involved.

Above: Nothing could be more stunning than a satsuki azalea bonsai in bloom. There are hundreds of varieties in a wide range of colours.

Above: In mid-summer, stewartia bonsai produce delicate, cup-shaped flowers which resemble those of their near relations, the camellias.

All about
BONSAI

What is a bonsai?

Most people are familiar with a bonsai's appearance, but what exactly is a bonsai? Not every tree grown in a pot will qualify as a bonsai. For a tree to be regarded as a bonsai, it must have certain defining characteristics: it must be grown in a container; it must have a distinctive artistic shape; and it must be miniature in size. A bonsai should be a small-scale replica in a pot of a fully grown tree that you might see in nature, its size and aesthetic appearance controlled by regular pruning, pinching and shaping, watering and feeding.

The 21 styles

The Chinese, who invented bonsai, still refer to them as artistic pot plants, which implies that bonsai are not simply plants in pots but also works of art. To qualify as a bonsai, a tree should conform to one of the distinctive bonsai styles. There are 21 principal shapes, which may be single-trunk, multi-trunk or multi-tree styles. The different formations range from the absolutely straight formal upright style and the S-shaped informal upright style (the most common of bonsai shapes) to the stripped-bark driftwood style,

Left: This trident maple is an excellent specimen, with a fine root buttress and tapered trunk and a natural appearance.

reminiscent of weathered mountain trees, and the broom style, which resembles a domed mop head and is the most natural looking of the bonsai styles. For more on shaping your bonsai tree, see pages 28–33.

Chinese beginnings

The art of bonsai has a rich and colourful history. It was the ancient Chinese who first practised the art more than two millennia ago. The word 'bonsai' derives from two Chinese words meaning a potted tree: *bon* (or *poon*) means pot and *sai* (or *sue*) means tree.

The Chinese have been growing ornamental plants for thousands of

Above: These Chinese elms make a good example of Chinese bonsai style. They have been planted in the penjing (landscape) style.

years – they were one of the earliest civilizations to do so. They also have a tradition for making fine ceramics, which dates back many thousands of years. It is not surprising that when these two arts were brought together the result was bonsai – plants grown in ceramic pots.

The Chinese loved the art of bonsai, but during the 1950s and until the 1980s it was nearly extinguished by the communist regime, which regarded growing bonsai as a revisionist and bourgeois pastime. It is only in the last few decades that the Chinese authorities have started to encourage the practice of bonsai again, and now it is once more a thriving and vibrant art form. For some

Above: This trident maple has been trained in the Japanese style, which is usually less ornamental than the Chinese approach.

people it is a pleasant and enthralling way to pass the time, but for others bonsai is big business, and almost all the indoor bonsai sold around the world today come from China.

Gradual Japanese differences

The Japanese are also involved in bonsai, but, contrary to popular belief, the practice did not originate in Japan. The Japanese started creating bonsai around the 12th century CE, almost a millennium after the Chinese first practised the art.

Chinese influences on Japan have been all-pervasive. The Japanese language itself, the Buddhist religion and art in general all have their origins in China. Zen Buddhism in particular, which has been such a key influence on Japanese culture, was introduced from China. Similarly, the arts of garden making and bonsai were imported from China. Although Japanese bonsai today are quite different from Chinese examples, it was not until the early 20th century that a distinctive Japanese style of bonsai began to emerge. Up to that time, Chinese and Japanese bonsai were indistinguishable.

Left: This driftwood yew is a good example of the emerging European style of bonsai.

Bonsai today

During the period following the Second World War when China was in turmoil, the Japanese began to develop bonsai in their inimitable style. The US occupying forces in Japan and the Japanese immigrant community in the USA then made bonsai more widely known in the West, and during the second half of the 20th century the interest in bonsai mushroomed.

Today, there is no corner of the world where bonsai are not grown. They have become established in most Asian countries, including India, Indonesia, Vietnam and Sri Lanka. They have also become popular throughout Europe

Above: Fuchsia can be made into effective bonsai. It is the shaping that introduces the difference between an ordinary shrub and an artistic pot plant.

and North America, and they are grown in Australia, Africa and South America. There is hardly a country today where the art of bonsai is not practised.

There is undoubtedly a unique Japanese style of bonsai and a unique Chinese one, but there are now also distinct European and North American styles, because each nation has interpreted the art of bonsai in its own way and stamped its imprint on the tradition. Each culture has learned to express its identity through the beauty of these miniature trees. This is why keeping bonsai is such a fascinating art and hobby.

Above: The autumn tints of Japanese maples are stunning.

Getting started

There are many ways of starting to keep bonsai, but the easiest is to buy a plant from a reputable nursery or specialist bonsai centre. However, before you do so, it is well worth finding out more about bonsai.

What is involved?

Bonsai keeping is quite a time-consuming pastime, and you should be prepared to water them on a regular basis if you want to keep your trees alive. Watering is by far the most important task because bonsai are always grown in containers (often shallow ones) and so depend entirely on their owner for their water supply. In summer, your bonsai will

Above: Special pots, like these handmade ones, are an integral part of bonsai. After all, a bonsai is by definition a tree in a pot.

need to be watered once or sometimes twice a day. Even in winter, when there is normally an ample supply of natural rain, bonsai that are kept outside require watering during dry spells, while indoor bonsai will need water all year round.

Before you go away on holiday you must make arrangements for the care of your bonsai. Some enthusiasts take their trees to a bonsai nursery, and others arrange for bonsai 'sitters' or 'minders' to look after their bonsai while they are away. Fortunately, the development of automatic irrigation systems has made both holiday and general watering care much easier.

Other important chores involved in bonsai care include pruning and pinching new shoots during the growing season. If your plants are vigorous, this can be a time-consuming task. (For more details on bonsai care, see pages 26– 41.)

Space

Space is another factor to think about before you make your first purchase. Although bonsai may be small in size, a collection of just a few trees can soon occupy all the available space in your garden. Many enthusiasts like to display their trees in authentic oriental garden settings, and this involves constructing suitable display areas to show off the trees. When this is done well, the bonsai look stunning. However, you would have to dedicate a large part of your garden to this type of arrangement – and that might not accord with the way the rest of your family would like to use the area.

Keeping indoor bonsai also requires some planning, because each tree needs to be placed in the best possible location for its particular requirements. Sunny windowsills and special growing areas are not always available, so consider carefully before you buy a large plant.

First steps

Joining a bonsai or gardening club, if there is one in your neighbourhood, is a good way to research bonsai and will be an invaluable source of advice about where and what to buy. Buying

Above: A display of accent or companion plants, used in bonsai displays, at an exhibition in Britain. Bonsai exhibitions are now quite common throughout the world.

on impulse is not a good idea, especially if your purchase is from a non-specialist centre such as a shopping mall, market stall or via the internet.

Exhibitions and competitions

Visiting exhibitions is an excellent way to see top-quality bonsai, while many nurseries and bonsai clubs put on splendid displays too. You can derive inspiration from the plants on display, and as you get drawn into the hobby you may want to exhibit your own plants. National bonsai organizations and local bonsai clubs will be able to give you more information about such events.

Choosing and buying bonsai

Most people buy their first bonsai because they think it is attractive or will suit their decor. But this is not a good basis on which to make a choice. If you are a beginner, you should select a species that is easy to keep and that is appropriate for the conditions you are able to offer.

Where to buy

The best place to buy bonsai and bonsai accessories is a specialist bonsai nursery. Finding sources should not be difficult if you have access to the internet, but take care before you purchase, as many so-called online 'specialists' are not experts at all. They are middle men who have little or no knowledge of bonsai. If you are making your first serious purchase, seek a second opinion about potential sources from a local bonsai club or horticultural society. Some large garden centres stock a good range of bonsai and may even have a resident expert to give you advice.

If you want to buy on the internet, make sure the firm is a reputable one. Download details of the address and telephone number, so that you can get in touch with the supplier if there are any problems. A specialist nursery, which gives personal advice, is always best, especially if you need aftercare service.

Department stores, shopping malls and hardware stores do not offer bonsai an ideal living environment, and trees sold from such outlets are rarely in good condition. The staff are also unlikely to know anything about growing and caring for bonsai.

Above: In a good bonsai nursery, you will be able to find bonsai of every species, shape, size, style and price.

Above: When buying bonsai, look for good-quality features such as visible surface roots.

Above: Ugly roots and bad trunk scarring reduce the value of this bonsai.

If you are a beginner, avoid attempting to grow a tree from seeds or cuttings. It is perfectly possible to grow bonsai this way (see pages 38–9), but it can be a long and sometimes tedious process.

Selecting a plant

MATCH A PLANT TO ITS DESTINATION: If you have a sunny garden or a living room that is bathed in sunlight every afternoon, look for species that appreciate this environment; avoid shade-loving plants, which will not thrive in direct sun. If your garden is near the sea, consider the salt-laden winds, which can damage delicate foliage.

GOOD-QUALITY PLANTS: The health and vigour of a tree should be prime considerations. A healthy tree will look fresh, and the leaves will be turgid and well coloured. Avoid plants with limp or shrivelled foliage and never buy a bonsai that looks sick, even if it is being offered at a knock-down price. If there is something wrong with it, the chances are that it may not recover, and when it dies you will have wasted your money.

OPTIMUM CHARACTERISTICS: As well as the health and vigour of the tree, you should evaluate its physical qualities. Look for a good trunk, which tapers gradually from a broad base to narrow apex, and has clearly visible surface roots, which radiate evenly from the trunk base. You should also select a plant with an elegant placement and arrangement of branches, and a fine branch structure. Depending on such qualities, two trees of a similar size can vary enormously in price. If possible, try to take someone who has experience of growing bonsai with you when wanting to acquire an expensive plant.

SEASON OF PURCHASE: If you are buying bonsai in spring or summer, the leaves on the possible plant should be green and the branches well covered. In autumn and winter bonsai will look less fresh, and deciduous trees will be changing colour before the leaves fall in autumn. Judging the health of a deciduous plant in winter can be difficult, because it will have shed all its leaves.

Above: Bonsai come in all shapes and sizes. This is a *mame* (miniature) cherry tree, 5cm (2in) high, while *shohin* (small) bonsia may be 20cm (8in) high.

Pricing bonsai

As well as its overall quality, how much you have to pay for your bonsai will depend on several other factors, including where you live; whether the bonsai is an indoor or outdoor type; the bonsai's country of origin; the species or variety; the size of the bonsai; and the age of the bonsai.

WHERE YOU LIVE: If you reside in China or Japan, where bonsai are grown commercially in vast numbers, a bonsai will be cheaper than in countries that have had to import these plants.

TYPE OF TREE: Indoor bonsai tend to be less expensive than outdoor (hardy) trees, because most come from China, where production costs are low. Imported outdoor trees are often sourced from Japan, where production costs are higher and the trees are of better quality. In addition, indoor trees are intended for the mass market and tend to be of poorer quality, and therefore cheaper, than the outdoor examples from Japan.

COUNTRY OF ORIGIN: Only two countries, Japan and China, have a sizeable export trade in bonsai. They are also grown commercially in Korea and Taiwan, but on a lesser scale.

SPECIES: As with all goods, there are fashions in bonsai. There was a time when *Picea jezoensis* (yezo spruce) and *Juniperus rigida* (needle juniper) were popular species. Now you are more likely to see *J. chinensis* (Chinese juniper). Similarly, *Rhododendron indicum* (satsuki azalea) enjoyed a huge vogue 20 years ago, but now they are less fashionable. Prices reflect what is in demand.

SIZE: Bonsai may be miniature trees, but they come in a huge range of sizes. The most common are bonsai that can be carried easily in one hand. Next in popularity are the bonsai that can be carried in two hands. Then there are trees that are 1m (3ft) or more high and need two people to lift them. There are even some examples that can only be moved by several people. At the other end of the size spectrum are the bonsai that are grown in thimble-size pots.The Japanese have names for all the different sizes, and bonsai exhibitions and competitions have strict criteria for judging the various categories. However, the amateur grower is less likely to be concerned with the different size categories than with the overall beauty of the tree. As a rule, the larger the bonsai, the

more expensive it will be. This is because the taller trees take longer to grow, require bigger, more expensive pots and cost more to transport. But size is not everything, of course, and a top-quality, small bonsai can cost more than a larger but poorer example of the same species.

AGE: As with size, age is also important in determining the price of a bonsai, and an older bonsai will be more expensive than a similar, younger example. Ultimately, however, the beauty of the plant is the overriding factor.

Above: This is a very old driftwood Chinese juniper bonsai. The age of the tree and the popularity of the style make it very valuable.

Outdoor and indoor bonsai

A common misconception about bonsai is that they have to be grown indoors. Many people regard them as delicate, fragile plants, which need to be protected from the elements. They tend to forget that bonsai are trees and that their natural environment is in the open. However, it is important to distinguish between outdoor and indoor bonsai as they require different growing conditions and care regimes.

Outdoor bonsai

Bonsai growers often regard the outdoor plants as the 'real' bonsai. These are the trees and shrubs that will grow outside without special protection. Many bonsai enthusiasts grow only outdoor bonsai because they are much easier to care for and there is more scope for creativity. As outdoor bonsai grow faster than

Above: Bougainvillea must be grown indoors in temperate regions, but make fine outdoor plants in tropical countries.

indoor bonsai, you will see the results of reshaping, wiring and pruning much sooner. Outdoor bonsai also offer more scope for practising the hobby. Some enthusiasts make their own bonsai from garden and nursery plants, and some collect the raw material from the wild. You can also propagate your own plants from seed or cuttings or by layering (see pages 38–9).

Outdoor bonsai can be taken indoors from time to time. In fact, in countries such as China and Japan, it is traditional to use bonsai to decorate the home, but the trees are kept indoors for only short periods. After a day or two they are returned to their outdoor positions.

The choice of outdoor bonsai is much wider than of indoor species. They tend to be more attractive than indoor trees, especially the deciduous and flowering subjects. Because they are easier to look after, outdoor bonsai live longer than indoor specimens. Indeed, some outdoor bonsai can live for more than a hundred years.

Indoor bonsai

Onc advantage of growing indoor bonsai is that many beginners like to keep their bonsai where it can be seen at all times. Bonsai are also useful for decorating a room, reflecting your taste and making a

What's the difference?

Most indoor bonsai are broad-leaved tropical and subtropical trees. Like *Ficus* (fig), many are also grown as houseplants, so are fairly easy to recognize. A few indoor species, such as *Podocarpus* and *Juniperus procumbens*, are coniferous and could be confused with hardy outdoor bonsai. Outdoor bonsai, on the other hand, are hardy species that grow naturally outside. Broad-leaved species, such as *Acer* (maple) and *Crataegus* (hawthorn), and conifers, such as *Pinus* (pine) and *Juniperus* (juniper), are not difficult to identify as outdoor plants.

statement about your lifestyle. In recent years, bonsai have become popular because they are associated with Zen and minimalist styles of decor.

The main drawback of indoor bonsai is that they are difficult to look after and may be short-lived if you do not provide the appropriate conditions. They need to be watered and fed regularly, and misted from time to time to provide a humid environment. They are also extremely demanding when it comes to ambient temperature, which must be constant. If you go away for a holiday or even a long weekend you will need to arrange for someone to look after your trees in your absence. Indoor bonsai are, in fact, like demanding pets.

Above: Figs, such as this Green Island fig, are among the easiest indoor bonsai to care for and will thrive in the interior.

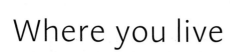

Where you live

An understanding of how plants are affected by climate and geography is essential to growing bonsai successfully. These pages are intended to help you understand the relationship between climate, geography and its influence on the cultivation of bonsai. Choosing the right type of plant for the climate zone in which you live is one of the key factors to successful bonsai culture.

Basic plant needs

All plants require air, sunlight and water for healthy growth. The availability of these ingredients is, therefore, crucial for the health of bonsai too. Air is needed by the roots and leaves to breathe. If the supply of air to the roots and leaves is restricted in any way, the plant will not grow well. Hence the importance of a well-aerated soil and free-flowing air for good, healthy growth. Water is another key ingredient. Given that more than 50 per cent of a plant's physical structure is made up of water, the availability of water is the prime factor for a plant's survival. Similarly, providing the right amount of water for your bonsai is key to keeping your bonsai alive. Finally, we must not forget the importance of light. Light is the source of food for plants, as it is the agent for photosynthesis.

Geography

Climate and environment determine the type and species of plants that grow in different parts of the world. Temperature, rainfall, humidity, sunlight and diurnal variations of sunlight (that is, day length) are other key factors. Soil type, altitude and protection from prevailing winds are also important. Local conditions sometimes create unique climatic variations, which are referred to as micro-climates, and these also determine what will or will not grow in each area.

Climate zones of the world

Latitude, altitude and proximity to oceans largely determine a region's climate. There are roughly six climatic zones on planet Earth: polar; temperate; Mediterranean; tropical; desert; and tundra. No zone is distinct, because zones merge as they transition from one to another. Except for the polar and tundra regions of the world, bonsai is grown in all the other climate zones. Even in the desert regions, such as the Californian and Nevada deserts, western Australia and southern Africa, some plants do thrive, and it is therefore not surprising that bonsai is practised there.

TEMPERATE ZONE: Plants that grow in the temperate zones of the northern and southern hemisphere are quite varied and include broad-leaved deciduous

and coniferous trees. This climate zone covers some parts of the US and Canada, much of Europe, Argentina, parts of southern Africa, Australia and New Zealand, and mountainous parts of China and Japan. It is characterized by mild temperatures and moderate rainfall. Trees that are typical of this region include the *Acer* (maple), *Fagus* (beech), *Fraxinus* (ash), *Juniperus* (juniper), *Larix* (larch) *Picea* (spruce), *Pinus* (pine), *Quercus* (oak) and *Ulmus* (elm) The temperate zone merges into the Mediterranean and subtropical regions where a large number of broadly similar species of trees and plants cohabit.

MEDITERRANEAN ZONE: This region is characterized by dry summers and rainy winters. Summers are hot in the inland regions, but cooler near the seas. Many of the trees and plants that grow in this zone have small, compact leaves with a waxy coating, to reduce moisture loss. *Eucalyptus* (gum), *Juglans* (walnut), junipers, Mediterranean oaks, *Olea* (olive) and pines are commonly found in Mediterranean areas, and many of them make excellent bonsai. Countries in this

Left: This ancient Mediterranean black pine, growing in the Troodos mountains of Cyprus, has developed into an interesting shape.

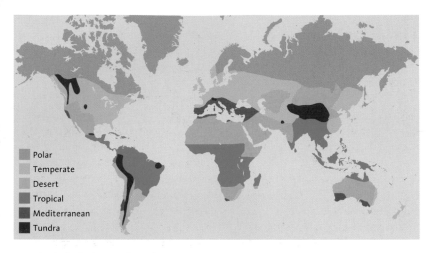

Polar
Temperate
Desert
Tropical
Mediterranean
Tundra

zone include Spain, southern France, Italy, western Turkey, Greece, Cyprus, Malta, Lebanon, Israel, Algeria, Morocco, Tunisia, California, parts of south Australia and Chile.

TROPICAL ZONE: The tropical zone surrounds the Equator, and lies typically within the Tropic of Cancer and the Tropic of Capricorn. The climate is warm and hot with heavy rainfall, although many tropical regions do have a dry and a wet season. The tropics are home to more than half of our planet's flora and fauna, so the range of trees and plants that grow in this zone is enormous, which makes them so exciting for bonsai – almost any species can be adapted to

Above: Bonsai can be grown in all except the tundra and polar climate zones of our planet.

bonsai culture. The abundant sunlight and copious rainfall mean that it is sheer paradise for plants. Most tropical plants are evergreen, broad-leaved species, and because they grow in warm, humid conditions they cannot withstand frosts and are therefore not suitable for growing outdoors in temperate climates. The plant species that grow in the Tropics are too numerous to mention individually. More than a hundred countries have a tropical climate, and they include India, Indonesia, Malaya, southern China, Brazil, parts of Australia, Chile and Kenya.

Plant hardiness zones

The plant hardiness zone system is another method used for classifying the ability of trees and plants to survive in different climate regions. This system is based on 12 zones, each with a specified minimum temperature in which certain plants thrive. Thus zone 1 is for plants that tolerate a minimum temperature of -51°C (-60°F), zone 2 has a minimum temperature of -40°C (-40°F), and so on. In zone 11 there is a minimum temperature of 10°C (50°F). This classification system is used quite widely in USA, Canada and Australia and has recently been introduced in the UK, but is hardly known in other countries. It is a very useful guide for checking a plant's ability to survive the minimum winter temperatures in the area in which it is intended to grow.

Environment for indoor bonsai

The trees and plants suitable for indoor cultivation are tropical and subtropical species, and the environment in which they grow needs to replicate as nearly as possible their native habitat. Unfortunately, the indoor environment in the temperate and Mediterranean regions can never be the same as that found in the tropics and subtropics, unless of course you provide a lot of artificial light and humidity. That is why indoor bonsai do not grow as well as their outdoor counterparts.

Above: Snow-covered slopes such as this are ideal habitats for coniferous trees and can be found almost anywhere in the world.

Above: This ancient banyan tree grows in eastern India in damp, humid conditions.

Looking after BONSAI

Structural shaping, pruning and pinching

The shapes of most bonsai are artificial. Even those bonsai that are collected from the wild, known as *yamadori* (a Japanese word meaning 'collected from the mountain'), require some shaping.

Tools

There are hundreds of different tools on the market for the bonsai hobbyist, ranging from twig- and branch-cutting implements to power tools for carving, and brushes for cleaning bark. For a beginner, all that is needed is a pair of ordinary garden secateurs or pruners, wire of different sizes, and a pair of pliers for cutting wire. Of the specialist bonsai tools, the most useful are the concave branch-cutter, the twig-pruning scissors, the root-pruning scissors and the root hook or rake. Other bonsai tools are useful but not essential for most growers.

Structural shaping

Hard pruning is done on an untrained tree or shrub to create the framework of the future bonsai, and on a tree that needs reshaping because it has lost its form. It is best undertaken in spring or mid-summer, when the tree will heal readily. Further refining the tree with wiring will make it look even better (see pages 31–3). It takes a trained eye to create a bonsai from an ordinary shrub; use pictures of good bonsai and tree shapes in nature as references.

Pruning

Ongoing light pruning and pinching are required on a regular basis, to keep your bonsai small and neat. Branches and stems are cut to refine or maintain the appearance of the tree. Light pruning also helps to make your bonsai healthier, allowing light to penetrate the inner branches, improving air circulation and helping to keep pests and disease to a minimum.

A deciduous tree usually needs to be pruned twice a year. Evergreen bonsai

Pruning branches

1 Use a concave branch-cutter or a saw to remove large branches, getting in as close as you can to the main trunk of the plant. The concave shape of this cutter ensures the remaining stub does not spoil the line of the trunk.

2 After removing a large branch of a non-resinous tree, seal the wound immediately with Japanese cut paste, available from bonsai stockists. Make sure all the edges are covered. The paste will fall off naturally as the wound heals.

do not require trimming as often, because they are usually less vigorous than deciduous trees.

Cut back to dormant buds to stimulate new shoots and the development of a good branch framework. Avoid cutting through any leaves or needles when pruning, because this will turn the tips brown.

Pruning flowering subjects is always a compromise between maintaining the shape of the bonsai and taking care to ensure that there will be an adequate supply of new buds for next year's flowers. The flowering buds are usually borne on the previous year's growth. If that is the case on your plant, pruning back too hard in summer will mean sacrificing the following year's crop of flowers. On the other hand, you should not let new shoots extend too far, because this will spoil the shape of the tree and inhibit the development of laterals – the secondary shoots that actually carry the flowering buds.

From time to time, you may need to let the tree have a rest, leaving shoots to grow unchecked so that the bonsai regains vigour. This is particularly true of deciduous species. Fruiting and flowering trees should be allowed to rest once every 3–4 years.

LEAF PRUNING: This is the total or partial defoliation of a deciduous bonsai. It is performed to introduce sunlight into the twig structure and induce a new crop of leaves, which will usually (though not always) be smaller in size and will emerge after four or five weeks. Leaf pruning should be done only on healthy trees or on those that have become dehydrated.

Pinching

This is the term for removing the growing tip of a new shoot, by using a pair of tweezers or your thumb and forefinger. It is done throughout the growing season to maintain the overall shape of the tree, and it must be carried out when new shoots are still soft. The tips of deciduous trees are usually pinched out when two or three new leaves appear, and pines are also controlled by selective removal of the 'candles' (new spring shoots).

Fortunately, pinching is not as onerous as it sounds, because shoots grow in spurts. Each year, a tree will produce

Above: Use your forefinger and thumb to pinch out pine candles as they elongate in late spring. Remove the strongest, and leave one or two in each cluster to develop.

new ones a limited number of times. Pines grow new candles once a year, whereas other evergreens and deciduous bonsai do so two or three times a year.

Trees grown principally for their foliage can be pinched quite freely, but those grown for their flowers need more care. You should not remove the flowering shoots that are usually borne on the tips of new shoots. Thus, on flowering subjects, pruning and pinching are not usually done after mid-summer, when the flower buds for the following year will have set. You can recognize potential flower buds by their plumpness. If the buds at the leaf axils are not plump, then in all probability they will be leaf buds.

Wiring

The use of wire in bonsai is similar to that of a brace for shaping children's teeth. By applying wire of the correct strength to a branch or trunk, the shape in which it is bent will set over a period of time. This modern way of styling bonsai is a convenient and quick method of achieving a desired shape. Before wiring was used, the ancient Chinese and Japanese practitioners created bonsai shapes by pruning and tying down the branches with bamboo sticks and weights.

Wire type and size

The wires used for bonsai are specially annealed (softened) iron, aluminium and copper wires. They come in different gauges to cater for a wide range of branch and trunk thicknesses. For the amateur, aluminium wire is the easiest to handle. Copper is used by professionals, because the wire holds better and is less obtrusive.

Judging the appropriate size of wire is largely common sense and comes with experience. If you use a gauge of wire

Above: Coil the wire at an angle of 45 degrees to the branch and anchor the end of the wire securely. Do not twist the wire too firmly or it will scar the tree.

Above: In the 'one wire, two branches' method, a single piece of wire links two adjacent branches, so that one acts as the anchor for the other.

that is too thin, then it will not be strong enough to do the job. If it is too thick, it could damage the branch. The optimum size will depend on the pliability and thickness of the branch, so test the stiffness of the branches before you choose your wire.

How to wire

Measure the branches you wish to wire and cut a piece of wire about 1½ times this length. Anchor the wire securely, by coiling it around the trunk or the parent branch, otherwise it will not be taut enough to bend the branch you wish to shape. Move along the branch from the anchored point, coiling the wire firmly and pulling the branch into the desired position. Do not trap needles or leaves under the wire. Work gently to avoid cracking; you may need to wire in stages, tightening the wire after a couple of weeks to bend the branch further. Thick coniferous branches can be wrapped with raffia to prevent them from snapping.

How long to leave the wire on will depend on how thick and old the branch is. Young, vigorous shoots can set in as little as five to six months. Thicker branches may take two or more years

Above: Some growers deliberately leave the shaping wires permanently embedded in the trunk or branch, in order to make it swell and thicken.

to retain a shape. If the wire is left on for too long it will leave a scar, although this is not necessarily detrimental, because the healed marks can lend character to the tree, making it look gnarled and old.

Keep an eye on the wires as the tree grows in summer; *Acer* (maple) scars particularly easily. To prevent damage and scarring to branches when removing wires, use bonsai wire cutters rather than try to uncoil long lengths of wire by hand. If scarring does occur, seal the wound with cut paste.

Guy wires

You can use a guy wire if a branch is too thick to be wired into position in the conventional way (thick deciduous branches are more prone to snapping than coniferous and are, therefore, not often wired in the conventional way), or if you do not want to disfigure the branch. However, there are some disadvantages to using guy wires: they tend to be unsightly and you cannot obtain twists and bends in the branch.

To set a guy wire, tie a strong piece of wire to a suitable point on the branch and secure it to the trunk or another strong branch below.

Jins and sharis

Bonsai driftwood carvings, which seek to replicate the hollow trunks and deadwood found on trees in nature, have become very popular in recent years, the world over. The fashion has been stimulated by the great Japanese bonsai artist Masahiko Kimura, whose carved masterpieces are sculptures in their own right.

Jin is the term for deadwood on a branch, while shari refers to a stripped-trunk effect. Jins and sharis can be made at any time of the year, although, in the case of *Pinus* (pine), avoid mid- to late summer, when the sap is rising. With other species, summer is the optimum time to make jins and sharis, because any scars and cuts will heal over quickly. Apply cut paste to the edges of the bark to facilitate healing.

Jins and sharis look best on thick trunks and branches, because the wood reduces to nothing if attempted on thin trunks and branches. Take great care when working with power tools, and do not attempt to use them unless you have had proper training. Protective gear such as face mask, safety helmet, gloves and gauntlets are absolutely essential, and bystanders should be careful too. Manual tools, such as chisels, are seldom used to do such work.

To achieve the authentic, white, bleached effect seen on some bonsai, apply lime sulphur or bleach to the dry, dead wood. Once the driftwood effect has been created, the wood should in any case be preserved by applying lime sulphur to the wood once or twice a year when the weather is dry.

Watering and feeding

All plants need water and nutrients to grow. Like any container-grown plants, bonsai have to be watered regularly and they also need to be supplied with nutrients during the growing season. One of the commonest causes of death in bonsai is poor watering. Remember that small pots dry out much faster than large ones and will need watering more often. However, do not water too much – few trees will survive with their roots in waterlogged compost.

Watering outdoor bonsai

You should usually begin to water outdoor bonsai when they start into growth in spring. Continue to water throughout the growing season, which in temperate areas is from early to mid-spring until early to mid-autumn.

Above: Bonsai like this forest group need to be heavily drenched to ensure that all the trees receive sufficient water.

If bonsai are left outside in winter, the moist air and rain are usually sufficient to keep them alive, but you should water if there has been no rain for several days.

In the growing season, water every day, or even twice a day if it is hot and dry. Water in the early evening if you are doing this once a day, or in the morning and evening if you are watering twice.

Using a garden hose or a watering can, water the entire tree – the rootball, foliage, trunk and branches. Drench the soil thoroughly by applying water to the rootball for a full ten seconds – leave it to soak through for a few minutes and then repeat the whole process until water seeps through the drainage holes of the container.

When watering flowering bonsai, take care not to splash water onto the petals of the flowers, which are easily marked.

Watering indoor bonsai

Indoor bonsai must be watered throughout the year, although they need more water in the growing season and less in the dormant period of autumn and winter. Use a small watering can, cup or glass. After watering, stand the container in a gravel- or pebble-filled shallow tray so that excess water drains from the compost and into the tray. The water that collects in the drip tray helps to keep the bonsai moist and creates a humid atmosphere around the tree.

Never leave indoor bonsai permanently in a deep bowl of water because this can rot the roots. A plant's roots have to take up oxygen from the soil around them, and if the soil is waterlogged the bonsai will eventually 'drown'.

Misting is advisable for indoor bonsai as well as watering if the room is very dry. Use a hand sprayer to create a fine spray of water particles, which will increase humidity. Misting an indoor tree in this way is not enough to water the tree.

Above: Fertilizer is available in solid or liquid form. Be careful to give the right amount, as overfeeding can be just as harmful as underfeeding.

If the bonsai become dusty, take the plant to the shower and wash off the dust with tepid water. In warm weather, take it outside and wash with a hose or watering can.

Feeding

Even more than other container-grown plants, bonsai must have nutrients at regular intervals because of the limited volume of soil in which they grow.

With most bonsai, fertilizer should be applied only during the growing season. If plants are given nutrients when they are not growing, the fertilizer will be wasted or it will encourage growth at the wrong time of year and cause stress to the tree.

Environment

If your tree is ailing, you may be keeping it in the wrong environment. Indoor bonsai can be put outdoors only in summer, and even outdoor bonsai need protection from extremes of heat and cold. If given too little light, your plant will not thrive; if too much sun, the leaves will scorch. Compost is also vital: it should have enough body to support the tree and must be free draining, so the roots can breathe.

Temperature and light

If you have only a few outdoor bonsai, keeping them near the wall of the house may be sufficient protection from sun and cold. In winter, move them to an unheated greenhouse. An unheated shed can also be used for brief periods.

Above: A shelter made of corrugated plastic sheeting is ideal for protecting your bonsai during the winter months.

The best position for most indoor bonsai is a windowsill with maximum light. They also need a constant temperature.

Compost

Many bonsai growers now use the Japanese soil Akadama, which is a clay granule that is free draining but moisture retentive. It can be mixed with humus and sand to suit local growing conditions. A good compost consists of peat, sharp sand and loam. The proportions of the three basic ingredients vary, depending on the genera. *Pinus* (pine) and *Juniperus* (juniper) need two parts sharp sand, one part peat and one part loam. Fruiting and flowering trees usually prefer a loamier soil, with up to 50 per cent loam. Include as much as 50–75 per cent peat (or peat substitute) for indoor bonsai.

Repotting

Bonsai should be repotted only when they are pot bound – that is, when the roots completely fill the pot. It is a misconception that they require frequent repotting and root trimming to keep them small. Frequency of repotting depends on how vigorous the species is (see individual plant entries for more details), on the warmth of the climate and on the tree's age. As a very general guide, bonsai less than 15 years old should be repotted every two to three years, while older trees need repotting every four to five years.

Time of year

Early spring is the best time for repotting outdoor bonsai: the trees are about to start into growth, and any cuts made to the roots will heal quickly and new roots will soon grow. Should a bonsai pot break in the middle of the growing season – if it is blown over or accidentally knocked – put it into a larger pot and wait until the following spring to repot the plant. Repot indoor bonsai in late spring, as early spring is too cold for disturbing their roots.

Above: This bonsai is clearly very pot bound. When the roots reach this condition, it is definitely time to repot the plant.

How to repot

Remove the pot and tease out the rootball with a rake or chopstick. Discard one-third of the compost from the rootball and cut off long roots with a pair of scissors. Replace the tree in its container and work fresh compost around its roots. Trees that are sick or in poor health should not be repotted, because cutting the roots will do more harm than good. Seek advice if in doubt.

Propagation

This is an enthralling and satisfying pastime and well worth the effort. There are three main methods by which you can increase your plants: by seeds, by cuttings and by layering. You can also extend your collection by acquiring mature nursery trees or by digging up trees from the wild or your own garden. Experimenting with the different methods of propagation can be great fun.

Above: Japanese maple seedlings grow easily from collected fresh seed.

Seeds

Conifers, such as *Pinus* (pine) and *Juniperus* (juniper), and deciduous genera, such as *Acer* (maple), grow easily from seed. Always use fresh seed, and buy from a reputable supplier. Most genera should be sown in autumn, in seed compost or good-quality multi-purpose compost. Leave the seed trays outside or in a cold frame while the seed germinates. When the first leaves have formed, probably in the following spring, plant the seedlings in individual pots. Let them grow on for at least a year before training them as bonsai plants.

Cuttings

Not all trees can be propagated from cuttings, but junipers, *Cryptomeria* (Japanese cedar) and *Chamaecyparis obtusa* (Hinoki cypress) are conifers that produce roots readily from stem cuttings. Pines and *Larix* (larch) do not grow well from cuttings. Among deciduous genera, maples and *Ulmus* (elm) are perhaps the easiest to propagate from cuttings, while *Prunus* (cherry) and *Fagus* (beech) are difficult.

Pros and cons of bonsai propagation

Why you should do it
- Propagation is inexpensive and requires little special equipment.
- It provides useful experience of working with trees.
- It does not matter if you fail because you will have lost little except time.
- You will have the satisfaction of growing your own trees from scratch.

Why you should not do it
- All methods require patience – you will not get immediate results.
- Propagation can be frustrating because it's a long and tedious process.
- The end results may not look like bonsai.

Layering

This ancient method, still practised throughout Asia, involves restricting the flow of sap to a branch by removing a ring of bark or by tying wire around it. The area is then wrapped in soil or moss and encased in a plastic bag to retain moisture. Within a few weeks or months, roots will emerge. When sufficient roots have formed, the branch can be severed to grow as a tree. The method quickly produces mature plants, and it is used for propagating *Carpinus* (hornbeam), *Chamaecyparis* (cypress) *Fagus* (beech), junipers, larches, *Malus* (crab apple), maples, *Salix* (willow) and *Tamarix* (tamarisk).

Using sharp, sterile tools, take cuttings each no thicker than a matchstick. Greenwood cuttings (from the soft tips of shoots) are taken in early summer. Ripewood cuttings of evergreen shrubs are started in late summer or early autumn, and hardwood cuttings from deciduous trees and shrubs are taken in late autumn or early winter.

Insert the cuttings in a mix of equal parts peat and sharp sand, or try different quantities to see what works best. Hormone rooting powder or liquid can speed up the rooting process, but is not essential.

Above: A heel cutting is a shoot attached to a 'heel' of the previous year's wood. For maples, these are more successful than cuttings severed just below a stem or leaf junction.

Problems

If you begin by choosing the right species and getting the best advice, you will have a head start with your bonsai. But sometimes, even if you lavish all possible care on them and do everything that is recommended, they can still succumb to pests, diseases or ill health. Using excessive fertilizers or chemical sprays can also cause problems.

Yellowing leaves and excessive leaf drop

This condition can be caused by inadequate light, too much or too little water, or pest infestation. Yellowing leaves can also be caused by chlorosis, a condition in which a plant is unable to absorb minerals due to factors such as low temperatures and waterlogging.

Pests

ADELGIDS: These white, aphid-like insects are active from the early spring and can multiply profusely and cause serious damage to conifers such as pine and larch. Most insecticides will kill this pest.

APHIDS: Sap-sucking, green, yellow, pink, black or white insects are often found on young shoots in spring. Small infestations can be removed by hand, or by jetting water at the plant. There are several appropriate organic insecticides,

including pyrethrum, derris and specialized soaps.

RED SPIDER MITE: These are often a problem with indoor bonsai, when foliage becomes mottled and yellow-brown in mid-summer, and the leaves then drop. They are minute, yellow-green mites, which crawl on fine, silk webbing on the undersides of leaves. To get rid of the mites, spray the leaves with a strong jet of water or use an appropriate insecticide. Red spider mites are not such a problem with outdoor bonsai.

SCALE INSECTS: These sap-sucking insects are protected by white or greyish, waxy shells. These insects are most vulnerable to insecticides, especially malathion, early in the year.

VINE WEEVILS: Adult weevils eat notches from the edges of leaves, but the main damage is done by the cream-coloured, C-shaped, legless larvae, which live in compost and eat a plant's roots. When repotting, search the compost for the larvae and kill any you find. The best control is to water pathogenic nematodes into the compost during late spring.

Diseases

FIREBLIGHT: Flowers die first, then leaves, then shoots. Fireblight occurs most frequently in periods of warm, wet weather. Remove and burn all infected plant material and disinfect all tools that have come into contact with the plant.

GALLS: These growths on leaves and stems are caused by bacteria. Remove the affected leaves and stems and dispose of them, preferably by burning.

MILDEW: This is a fungal problem, which takes the form of a white, powdery growth on leaf surfaces. If unchecked, it will spread to stems and even the entire plant. To reduce the opportunities for an attack, direct water to the compost when watering bonsai and take care not to splash the leaves. Remove and burn infected foliage at once and, if necessary, spray with a suitable fungicide.

PEACH LEAF CURL: An attack of peach leaf curl is probable if new leaves look puckered and blistered in spring and a layer of white spores appears on the leaf surface. The leaves then drop, but are usually followed by a second flush of leaves. Pick off and burn affected leaves, and prevent the problem arising by keeping the tree under cover in spring so that the spores cannot reach the tree.

Above: Aphids are always a problem in early spring. They can do a lot of damage to the new leaves.

Above: Oak leaf gall will not harm your bonsai, but it looks extremely unsightly.

Outdoor coniferous BONSAI

Introduction

Nearly all conifers are evergreen, and evergreen trees have always had a special place in oriental folklore and culture. They symbolize longevity and timelessness, which is why *Pinus* (pine) and *Juniperus* (juniper) are favourite subjects in Chinese paintings and other works of art, including bonsai. Most gardeners, including bonsai enthusiasts, cultivate evergreen species because they provide interest in the form of colour and structure all year round.

Evergreen and deciduous

Some of the most popular evergreen conifers used for bonsai are *Cedrus* (see pages 46– 7), *Chamaecyparis* (see pages 48– 51), *Cryptomeria japonica* (see pages 52– 3), *Juniperus* (see pages 54– 71), *Picea* (see pages 76– 7) and

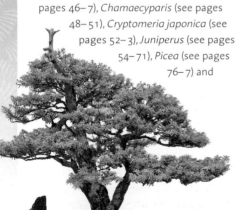

Pinus (see pages 78– 89). *Larix* (see pages 72– 3) and *Metasequoia glyptostroboides* (see pages 74– 5) are deciduous conifers.

Care of conifers

Evergreen trees are generally slower growing than deciduous species. The different growth habits of evergreen and deciduous species require a range of training techniques, and the wiring, pruning, pinching and even watering practices used for evergreens differ slightly from those needed for deciduous trees (see pages 26– 35).

All conifers produce cones in due course. On a bonsai these are no smaller than

Left: This northern Japanese hemlock is grown in a natural style and planted in a contemporary container.

44

Above: Each species used for bonsai has its own very distinctive characteristics, such as the twisted radial needles of dwarf mountain pine.

those on a full-size tree. However, do not allow too many cones to remain on a bonsai, because this can stress the tree.

In general, evergreen coniferous bonsai are perhaps a little easier to care for than deciduous ones, because they lose less water through their leaves in hot weather – the surface area of the leaves or needles being smaller than that of deciduous trees. Should you forget to water your pine or juniper on a hot summer's day, the chances are that it will not suffer from dehydration. The same could not be said for an *Acer* (maple) or *Fagus* (beech) tree. For this reason, a newcomer to bonsai might be wise to choose a pine or juniper as a first tree rather than a broad-leaved species.

Popular conifers for bonsai

Pines and junipers are the most popular evergreens for bonsai, and each genus contains many species and cultivars that offer enthusiasts a wide range of shapes and colours.

In Japan, *Pinus parviflora* (see pages 80– 1) and *P. thunbergii* (see pages 88– 9) are the two favourite species of pine. Elsewhere, *P. mugo* (see pages 78– 9) and *P. sylvestris* (see pages 86– 7) are particularly popular. When grown as bonsai, in other words when constrained within a small container, most pines develop shorter needles and internodes. As it ages, pine bark becomes fissured and gnarled, adding character to the tree.

There are similarly many species of juniper that are suitable for bonsai. *Juniperus chinensis* (see pages 56– 61) alone has given rise to scores of cultivars that can be used. Some of these have adult or cord-like foliage, while in others the foliage is juvenile or prickly. There are other juniper species that are popular with bonsai growers, including *J. communis* (see pages 62– 3), *J. procumbens* (see pages 64– 5), *J. rigida* (see pages 66– 7) and *J. squamata* (see pages 70– 1).

Cedrus

Cedar

- *hardy*
- *evergreen*
- *slow growing*
- *easy to keep*

All four species of cedar – *Cedrus atlantica* (Atlas cedar), *C. brevifolia* (Cyprus cedar), *C. deodara* (deodar) and *C. libani* (cedar of Lebanon) – make attractive bonsai. They have compact needles borne in clusters, the needles of Cyprus cedar being particularly small. Except for plants in the *C. atlantica* Glauca Group, which have blue needles, cedars have green foliage. They are easy to train as bonsai in most of the recognized styles and are quite widely used by European and Japanese enthusiasts. Unfortunately, not many commercial bonsai nurseries produce or stock them.

Where to keep them

Most cedars (zone 6) are native to countries in and around the Mediterranean. Deodar, however, is from the western Himalayas, where it grows at high altitudes, almost at the snow line. Cedars are hardy plants in temperate climates and do not require protection in winter. They can be kept in full sun throughout the year.

How to look after them

REPOTTING: Repot cedars in spring every 2–3 years into free-draining, alkaline, multi-purpose compost consisting

Above: The needles of cedar bear a striking resemblance to those of larch. Cedar, however, is coniferous, while larch is a deciduous genus.

of equal parts loam, peat (or garden compost) and sharp sand. Cedars do not tolerate waterlogged soil.

PRUNING AND PINCHING: Prune back branches in spring and autumn, cutting strongly growing branches back hard in autumn. When pruning, cut just above a cluster of needles, taking care not to slice through the needles. Pinch out the tips of new shoots with your fingers in spring and again in summer if necessary.

WIRING: Cedars can be wired at any time of the year and the wires left in place for up to 12 months, although check from time to time to make sure that the wire is not cutting into the bark.

WATERING: Like most coniferous trees, cedars do not transpire as much as their deciduous counterparts and are therefore able to withstand drought much better. Nevertheless, you should water regularly from spring to early autumn and occasionally in winter during dry spells.

FEEDING: Cedars benefit from a light feed of a high-nitrogen fertilizer in early spring. Follow this with 2–3 applications of a general fertilizer in summer.

BE AWARE: Although generally trouble free, cedars are susceptible to honey fungus, which must be treated with a fungicide as soon as symptoms are noticed. Pick off caterpillars by hand as soon as they appear.

Cedrus atlantica

Chamaecyparis obtusa

Hinoki cypress

- *hardy*
- *evergreen*
- *quite fast growing*
- *lush, green foliage*

Chamaecyparis obtusa (Hinoki cypress) and *C. pisifera* (Sawara cypress; see pages 50–1) are important timber trees in Japan, and the dwarf forms and cultivars of these make interesting bonsai subjects. Hinoki cypress has bright green foliage, arranged in whorls along the branches, and attractive, reddish-brown bark. Sawara cypress bears quite different needles (either prickly or soft and feathery), and its colours can range from gold to steel-blue, although most forms have bright green foliage.

Cypress bonsai are grown mainly in the formal upright style, and good specimens can be very expensive. Examples can be imported from Japan under special licence, in the same way that *Pinus parviflora* (see pages 80–1) and *Juniperus* (see pages 56–71) specimens can be.

Where to keep them

The Hinoki cypress is native to southern Japan and is normally hardy in temperate areas, although plants may need some protection in a frost-free shed or greenhouse if winter temperatures fall below -5°C (23°F). Hinoki cypress will

Above: The fan-shaped foliage of Hinoki cypress makes it a very attractive subject for bonsai.

happily survive when placed in full sun
throughout the growing season.

How to look after them

REPOTTING: These fairly vigorous trees
need repotting every other year, in late
spring. Use Akadama soil on its own or
a mix of equal parts of loam, peat
(or garden compost) and sharp sand.

PRUNING AND PINCHING: Prune back
secondary branches in spring or summer.
Pinch out new shoot tips two or three
times during the growing season.

WIRING: This should be done in
spring or mid-summer, taking care
not to trap foliage under the wire.
The wires should not be left in place
for longer than ten months and should
be replaced if necessary.

WATERING: Water Hinokis regularly
from spring to early autumn and
occasionally in winter during dry spells
so that the compost remains moist.
Mist plants from time to time in
summer, but ensure that the needles are
not scorched by droplets in sunlight.

FEEDING: Apply a high-nitrogen fertilizer
in early spring, followed by two further
doses of a general fertilizer in summer.

Chamaecyparis obtusa

BE AWARE: Hinokis are susceptible to scale
insects, which can be controlled by hand
if you notice them quickly or by applying
a systemic insecticide. They also lose a lot
of their old foliage in autumn, which can
be disconcerting for first-time growers.
When this happens, simply remove the
brown foliage by hand; the tree will then
look as good as new.

Chamaecyparis pisifera

Sawara cypress

- *suitable for most styles*
- *foliage needs frequent attention to look good*
- *easy to propagate from cuttings*
- *popular with hobbyists*

This Japanese timber tree has numerous cultivars, many of which make excellent bonsai. *Chamaecyparis pisifera* 'Boulevard' (Boulevard false cypress) and cultivars with 'Plumosa' in their name are popular because they are easy to train and shape. Sawara cypress foliage is attractive but needs a lot of grooming to keep it looking fresh. Like most evergreen conifers, sawara cypress leaves turn reddish brown with the onset of winter but revert to green again in spring. It is not often used commercially for bonsai.

Above: Sawara cypress foliage is awl-shaped and prickly. Some cultivars are green, while others (such as this 'Boulevard') are bluish grey.

Where to keep them

Sawara cypress (zones 4–7) is a hardy tree. Keep in full sun from spring to autumn but provide some protection from hard frosts in winter.

How to look after them

REPOTTING: Repot in spring every 2–3 years. Remove no more than a third of the roots when repotting. Sawara cypress is not fussy about soil, although it is best to use free-draining compost with lots of organic matter.

PRUNING AND PINCHING: Prune and pinch throughout the growing season, because this species is vigorous. When pruning, avoid cutting the foliage, because this leaves brown marks; it is better to cut into the wood instead.

WIRING: Sawara cypress can be wired at any time. Remove wires if they begin to bite into the wood. Never leave wires on for more than a couple of years.

WATERING: Apply lots of water in summer. The foliage can be drenched as well.

FEEDING: Feed in spring with a high-nitrogen fertilizer. Apply a low-nitrogen feed in late summer.

BE AWARE: Watch out for scale insects; treat with an appropriate insecticide. Remove the dead foliage regularly.

Chamaecyparis pisifera

51

Cryptomeria japonica

Japanese cedar, Sugi

- *hardy*
- *evergreen*
- *requires a lot of attention*
- *more challenging*

Japanese cedar is another Japanese tree that, together with its many cultivars, is now extensively used for bonsai. It has a fairly upright, columnar habit, fibrous red-brown bark, dark green foliage, which sometimes turns rusty-brown in winter, and brown cones. Because it tends naturally to have a straight trunk, this species is ideal for training in the formal upright style. Untrained nursery material is not difficult to obtain, but Japanese cedar bonsai is usually found only in good bonsai nurseries. Fine specimens tend to be expensive and are only rarely available.

Where to keep them

This hardy species (zones 5–6) from Japan can be kept outdoors all year round. However, the foliage tends to turn brown in prolonged periods of very cold weather (although it reverts to green in spring). To avoid this, you can move your

plant to a frost-free shed or greenhouse. Japanese cedar does best in a bright but partially shaded position in summer.

How to look after them

REPOTTING: Repot Japanese cedar every other spring into free-draining but moisture-retentive compost consisting of equal parts Akadama soil (or loam) and sharp sand. Alternatively, use one part leaf mould and one part loam to one part sharp sand.

Left: The new foliage grown by Japanese cedar needs to be pinched back constantly to prevent it from becoming coarse.

PRUNING AND PINCHING: Japanese cedar requires constant grooming to keep it looking its best. Begin to prune in late spring and continue during the growing season. Finish with a light pruning in autumn. Remove unwanted shoots from the trunk and main branches, and cut back shoots that are beginning to look bare. Regularly pinch out new shoot tips with your fingers, throughout summer.

WIRING: Wire Japanese cedar in spring or early summer, taking care not to trap foliage under the wire. Remove the wires when they become too tight or if you are worried about marking the branches.

WATERING: These plants require a lot of water in order to grow well. In summer, you need to water at least twice a day, and if you neglect to water properly branches may suffer from die-back. In winter, keep the compost moist but not too wet and avoid watering in frosty weather. During summer, mist plants frequently, to increase the humidity around the needles.

FEEDING: In early summer apply a high-nitrogen fertilizer and in early autumn apply a general fertilizer.

BE AWARE: The dense foliage can harbour scale insects and red spider mites, although constant thinning will help to keep these to a minimum. Remove them by hand or jetting with water, or apply a weak systemic insecticide.

Cryptomeria japonica

Juniperus californica

California juniper

- *iconic species*
- *dream tree*
- *best for warm Mediterranean climates*
- *stunning driftwood effects*

Of all the tree species used for bonsai in America, California juniper is the iconic one! It is one of about 60 or so species of the *Juniperus* genus, and its native habitat is the Californian, Nevada and Arizona deserts. The hot, arid growing conditions of its native habitat make it difficult for California juniper to survive outside these areas. Like *J. chinensis* 'Shimpaku' (see pages 58–9), it is sought after by bonsai enthusiasts for its gnarled and twisted trunk. The foliage is a bit coarse, unlike *J. chinensis* 'Itoigawa' (see page 59).

The best bonsai are made from trees collected from the wild. Young plants are difficult to obtain, as they are challenging to grow from seed or cuttings. In any case, young plants lack the dramatic driftwood that older specimens have. Good examples of California juniper are as highly prized as *J. chinensis* 'Itoigawa'. Should you be so lucky as to own one, take extra care in maintaining it – this species is not for the novice. Get advice on how to look after it from a local expert.

Where to keep them

If grown in zones 8–10, California juniper tolerates moderate frosts on cold winter nights. Elsewhere, protect it in the winter

Left: The berries of California juniper are a rich source of food for wildlife.

from hard frosts. It likes full sun for most of the year except in the hottest summer months, when it needs shade.

How to look after them

REPOTTING: Repot every 3–4 years, using very gritty, free-draining compost consisting of one part grit (or sharp sand) and one part loam (or Akadama). Spring is usually the best time, but some experienced growers like to pot in autumn. Be careful not to cut off too much root when repotting.

PRUNING AND PINCHING: Prune when the young strong shoots emerge in early summer. Do this with a pair of sharp scissors, rather than by pinching.

WIRING: California juniper can be wired at any time of the year.

WATERING: Although it likes to kept on the dry side, some water is of course needed. Never drown or overwater this species. California juniper prefers having its foliage misted for most of the year.

FEEDING: California juniper does not require much feeding, but a general fertilizer in spring and summer will help to green up the foliage.

BE AWARE: Watch out for the pests, such as scale insects and red spider mite; treat with appropriate insecticides. As pear rust can sometimes be a problem with junipers, avoid growing them near any of the Rosaceae family as a precautionary measure.

Juniperus californica

Juniperus chinensis

Chinese juniper

- *hardy*
- *evergreen*
- *easy to keep*
- *attractive foliage*
- *eye-catching bark*

Of the various types of juniper that can be used for bonsai, Chinese juniper and its many cultivars are preferred by most bonsai enthusiasts. The species itself has deep green, cord-like foliage and red-brown bark; mature specimens develop gnarled and twisted trunks. Most important of all, Chinese juniper is extremely hardy and easy to keep. It is suitable for all bonsai styles.

Where to keep them

Chinese juniper (zones 4–8) is native to China and Mongolia, and it is hardy in all temperate areas of Europe, requiring no special protection in winter. In North America it should not be regarded as entirely hardy, and in areas where temperatures fall below -10°C (14°F), plants should be moved to a frost-free shed or greenhouse in winter. Although Chinese juniper can be kept in full sun, some enthusiasts prefer to cover it with shade netting, which not only improves the colour of the foliage but also protects the plant from extremes of heat and cold.

Above: The foliage of older, pot-bound Chinese juniper becomes adult or cord-like. There are many cultivars – Itoigawa juniper (*Juniperus chinensis* 'Itoigawa') is shown here.

How to look after them

REPOTTING: When it becomes pot bound, which could be every 3–4 years or longer, repot Chinese juniper in early spring. Never remove more than one-third of the rootball when repotting. It needs free-draining compost of one part Akadama soil (or loam), one part humus (or peat) and two parts sharp sand. Or try equal parts of loam, leaf mould and sharp sand.

PRUNING AND PINCHING: There is no need to remove the main branches of an established Chinese juniper, unless you are reshaping the tree. In that case, cut right back into the woody growth, but avoid cutting through the foliage, because this will make the tips brown. Maintain the overall shape of the tree from early spring to autumn by pinching out the growing tips of the new shoots with your fingers. The aim is to keep the foliage dense and tight, so avoid letting new shoots grow too long.

WIRING: This can be done at any time of year, taking care not to trap foliage under the wire. Do not leave the wires on for longer than necessary, and do not let them bite into the bark.

WATERING: Water your bonsai regularly from spring onwards, starting with once a day in spring and early summer and increasing to twice daily in mid-summer. Towards the latter part of summer and into autumn,

water once a day. In winter, keep the soil just moist. Never let the soil become waterlogged or dry out completely.

FEEDING: In early spring, apply a high-nitrogen fertilizer. Continue feeding throughout summer by applying a general fertilizer every two months until autumn.

BE AWARE: Chinese juniper attracts scale insects. Use appropriate insecticides to get rid of them.

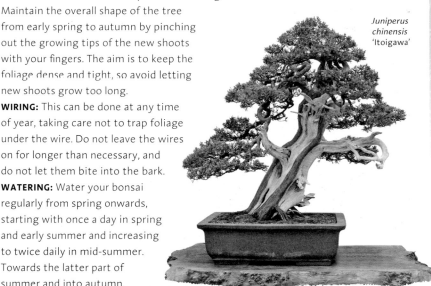

Juniperus chinensis 'Itoigawa'

Juniperus chinensis 'Shimpaku'

Chinese juniper varieties 1

- *easy to keep*
- *evergreen conifer*
- *attractive green foliage*
- *stunning driftwood effects*

Much of the innovation in bonsai since the 1970s and 1980s has been centred around *Juniperus chinensis*. It is probably one of the single most-sought-after evergreen species for any bonsai hobbyist or collector. A good-quality Chinese juniper commands some of the highest prices for bonsai. However, its nomenclature is misunderstood – in particular the term 'Shimpaku'.

'Shimpaku' may be regarded as a subspecies of *J. chinensis*. The variety that most closely resembles 'Shimpaku' is *J. chinensis* 'Globosa Cinerea', because it also has cord-like foliage. Some Japanese bonsai manuals refer to 'Shimpaku' as *J. chinensis* var. *sargentii*, which is a prostrate form of juniper from the northern islands of Japan. However, this bears little resemblance to the 'Shimpaku' that is used by bonsai growers in Japan and China. The Chinese refer to 'Shimpaku' as 'Ying Pak' ('true cypress'). The term 'Shimpaku' came into use in the late 19th century in Japan, when Japanese bonsai traders referred to 'Shin-Paku' ('new cypresses or cypress'). These juniper trees were collected from the mountains and fetched high prices.

Above: The eye-catching driftwood effects show well in this large Itoigawa juniper.

'ITOIGAWA': By far the most highly prized of all the 'Shimpaku', this has very fine, cord-like, mid-green foliage. Its gnarled and twisted trunks and branches lend themselves to dramatic driftwood effects such as jins and sharis (see page 33). Young branches can also be wired

Juniperus chinensis 'Itoigawa' *Juniperus chinensis* 'Kishu'

Juniperus chinensis 'Tohoku'

into these shapes. 'Itoigawa' responds well to pruning, as it buds back easily. It originates from the Itoigawa region of Japan in the Niigata prefecture. For much of the late 19th and early 20th centuries, 'Itoigawa' from the wild mountains was the main source of the famous exquisite juniper specimens. Collectors risked life and limb to seek these trees – hence the mystique surrounding 'Itoigawa'. This variety is now used extensively in commercial bonsai nurseries.

'KISHU': The most common variety of the 'Shimpaku' juniper to be grown and sold commercially is *J. chinensis* 'Kishu'. The foliage is slightly coarser than that of 'Itoigawa'. Its colour is deep green but can vary depending on the feed used.

'TOHOKU': This 'Shimpaku' variety originates in the Tohoku region of Japan.

Its trunk, bark and driftwood effects are similar to those of 'Kishu', while its foliage is coarser and floppy. The leaves and twigs require much wiring. *Juniperus chinensis* 'Tohoku' tends to produce a lot of seed, which spoils the look of the foliage.

Juniperus chinensis cultivars

Chinese juniper varieties 2

- *easy to keep*
- *evergreen conifer*
- *attractive green foliage*
- *stunning driftwood effects*

For the bonsai enthusiast, the Chinese juniper is not just the 'Shimpaku', because there is a range of varieties and cultivars. The differences are mainly in the foliage and trunk characteristics, which have a very significant effect on the appearance of the bonsai.

Juniperus chinensis 'Blaauw'

'BLAAUW': *Juniperus chinensis* 'Blaauw' was introduced to Europe from Japan by the Dutch nursery Blaauw & Co. more than a century ago and has been used by bonsai hobbyists in the UK and the rest of Europe for the past 40–50 years. It is sold as an ornamental garden conifer and is, therefore, readily available. This Chinese juniper is easy to make into a bonsai. The bonsai (left) was created by the author in 1986 using ordinary garden-centre stock. The foliage of this cultivar has a bluish tinge when grown in the open ground, but, when used in a bonsai pot, the leaves turn mid-green, like all other commercial Chinese junipers. Bonsai created from 'Blaauw' is almost indistinguishable from that of *J. chinensis* 'Kishu' (see page 59).

Above: *Juniperus chinensis* 'Kaizuka'

'KAIZUKA': The foliage of *Juniperus chinensis* 'Kaizuka' (Hollywood juniper) bears a slight resemblance to Californian juniper. This cultivar is used extensively in California as a landscape tree, and hobbyists there have successfully adopted it for bonsai; some fine examples are to be found. Hollywood juniper is also popular in Japan for making *niwaki* (garden trees). It is not as popular for bonsai as some other varieties of *J. chinensis*, which have better foliage and growth habit.

Above: *Juniperus chinensis* 'Kaizuka'

Above: *Juniperus chinensis* 'Blaauw'

Above: *Juniperus chinensis* 'Tohoku'

Above: *Juniperus chinensis* 'Kishu'

Juniperus communis

Common juniper

- *hardy*
- *evergreen*
- *easy to keep*
- *gnarled trunk*
- *black fruit*

This evergreen shrub or small tree is an ideal species for bonsai. It has dark green to blue-green prickly needles, borne in threes, and spherical fruits, which ripen to black. There are several prostrate cultivars, including *Juniperus communis* 'Hornibrookii' and *J. communis* 'Repanda', as well as many dwarf and slow-growing forms. Plants eventually develop a gnarled, twisted trunk, which makes them ideal for driftwood. They are excellent subjects for bonsai shaped in a contemporary sculptural style.

The best examples of common juniper bonsai come from wild-grown plants. Unfortunately, common juniper is not used commercially and is not widely available. Good specimens are usually found in private collections.

Where to keep them

Common juniper (zones 2– 7) occurs naturally throughout much of the northern hemisphere, where it is perfectly hardy in temperate areas. In areas where temperatures fall below -10°C (14°F), move it to a frost-free shed or greenhouse in winter. It does best if it is placed in full sun throughout the growing season.

How to look after them

REPOTTING: Repot common juniper every 2– 3 years from mid- to late spring, but only if the tree is pot bound.

Above: Common juniper grows wild throughout Europe. It is an excellent plant for bonsai and resembles *Juniperus rigida* 'Yatsubusa' (dwarf needle juniper), which is found in Japan.

When doing so, never remove more than one-third of the rootball. It needs free-draining, slightly alkaline compost consisting of one part Akadama soil (or loam), one part peat (or garden compost) and two parts sharp sand.

PRUNING AND PINCHING: Prune back branches and old shoots in late spring, cutting back into the woody growth. Prune just above a cluster of needles, taking care not to slice through the needles themselves. Maintain the shape from early spring to autumn by pinching out the growing tips of new shoots with your fingers. The aim is to keep the foliage dense, so do not let new shoots grow too long.

WIRING: This can be done between the months of early spring and autumn. Be careful not to trap needles under the wire, and do not leave the wires in place for more than a year.

WATERING: Water common juniper regularly but sparingly, giving the plant more water in summer than in spring or autumn. In winter, keep the compost just moist. This plant will not thrive in waterlogged soil.

FEEDING: Start feeding the plant in early spring with a high-nitrogen fertilizer. In summer, apply a general fertilizer every couple of months. Do not feed common juniper in autumn or winter.

BE AWARE: Common juniper needs little special care. Sap-sucking insects can usually be dislodged by a jet of water or by hand. If they are persistent, apply a systemic insecticide. Exposure to frost temporarily turns common juniper yellow or brown.

Juniperus communis

63

Juniperus procumbens

Procumbens juniper

- *hardy*
- *evergreen*
- *easy to grow and style*
- *prone to scale insects*
- *used mainly for the cascade style*

This is a ground-hugging, creeping juniper originating in Japan but hybridized extensively for use as an ornamental plant. Some hybrids have been developed for tropical and subtropical climates. Its creeping habit makes procumbens juniper particularly good for the cascade style of bonsai. It is popular with hobbyists because it is easy to train, and is readily available in nurseries and garden centres.

Above: The colour of procumbens juniper foliage ranges from steel-blue to mid-green, depending on the fertilizer used.

Where to keep them

Procumbens juniper (zones 5–9) likes full sun, but can turn yellow if left in strong sunshine during the summer. If this happens, place the plant in partial shade during very hot weather. Plants developed for temperate climates are generally hardy, but those that have been grown in the tropics need protection from winter cold.

How to look after them

REPOTTING: Repot Procumbens juniper every 3–4 years, when pot bound, in early spring. Use a free-draining mix of one part Akadama soil (or loam), one part humus (or peat) and two parts sharp sand.

PRUNING AND PINCHING: Pinch or prune new growth at regular intervals, to keep the bonsai looking smart. Pruning may be better, provided you do not cut through any foliage, because this leaves brown marks on the tips.

WIRING: Procumbens juniper may be wired at any time of the year.

WATERING: It likes more moisture than other juniper varieties. When grown in a cascade style, there is a smaller surface area of compost than in a rectangular or oval pot, so take more care when watering.

FEEDING: Feed during the growing season with a high-nitrogen fertilizer in very early spring. Cease feeding by late summer.

BE AWARE: As some imported plants may originate from tropical Asia, they may need winter protection. Dead foliage needs regular cleaning. Some procumbens junipers in Europe, such as *J. procumbens* 'Nana', are prone to branch die-back. This could either be due to a viral disease or juniper blight. Cut out or burn infected branches or the entire plant when this occurs.

Juniperus procumbens

Juniperus rigida

Needle juniper, Temple juniper, Tosho

- *hardy*
- *evergreen*
- *fast growing*
- *gnarled trunk*
- *purplish berries*

The sharp, bright green needles, which make this species difficult to handle, are borne in groups of three on this spreading tree. Needle juniper produces purplish berries, and has peeling, brown bark and a gnarled trunk, which makes it a suitable species for driftwood. It is an easy-to-grow species, but requires a lot of pruning and pinching if it is to look its best. The tree is a great favourite with bonsai enthusiasts, and is fairly easy to obtain from bonsai nurseries in countries that permit its importation.

Where to keep them

Needle juniper (zone 6) is native to northern China, Korea and Japan. It is fully hardy in temperate areas. Where winter temperatures fall below -10°C (14°F), move needle juniper to a frost-free shed or greenhouse. It grows best in full sun during the growing season.

How to look after them

REPOTTING: Repot needle juniper every 2–3 years during mid- to late spring. Never remove more than one-third of the rootball. Repot in a free-draining,

gritty compost, such as a mix of equal parts Akadama soil (or loam) and coarse

Above: Most junipers bear fruit on all plants, but needle juniper is dioecious (the male and female plants are distinct) and only female plants will produce berries.

grit. Some Japanese nurseries plant needle juniper in pure grit.

PRUNING AND PINCHING: Prune old wood in early spring. Cut just above a cluster of needles, taking care not to cut through the needles themselves. When the new shoots start into growth in late spring, regularly prune and pinch out the growing tips with your fingers. Remove shoots emerging from the trunk and do not allow any shoots to grow too long.

WIRING: Needle juniper can be wired any time from autumn to early spring, taking care not to trap needles under the wire. Wires on thicker branches may need to be left in place for two or more years for the shape to set. Wrap the branch in raffia if it is very thick and in danger of snapping.

WATERING: Water regularly throughout the growing season, increasing the amount given in summer. Allow the surface of the soil to dry slightly between waterings. Although the compost must never be allowed to dry out completely, it is important that the soil never becomes waterlogged in winter, or the roots will rot. This applies to both indoor and outdoor trees.

FEEDING: Apply a high-nitrogen fertilizer in early spring and a general one in summer. Feed once a month. Do not fertilize during autumn and winter.

Juniperus rigida

BE AWARE: Scale insects and red spider mites can be a problem for needle juniper. Jetting plants with water usually removes the pests, but serious infestations should be treated with a systemic insecticide. Bear in mind that exposure to frost turns junipers temporarily yellow or brown.

67

Juniperus sabina

Sabina juniper, Savin

- *iconic evergreen*
- *stunning driftwood*
- *needs winter protection in temperate climates*
- *slow grower*

Sabina juniper grows wild throughout the Mediterranean region and in western Asia, where it develops a gnarled, twisted trunk and stunning driftwood, which makes beautiful natural bonsai. The foliage is a lovely green, and the branches are easy to wire. No wonder it has become such a popular species for bonsai. This species has hybidized with other junipers, such as *J. chinensis* to produce *J.* x *pfitzeriana*, but the hybidized garden plants do not have the beautiful, twisted trunks that are so characteristic of wild sabina junipers.

Unfortunately, sabina juniper is not produced commercially, and almost all sabina bonsai that are sold commercially are made from trees that are collected from the wild. Many are sourced from the Alps and mountainous regions of Europe, while others are found in the coastal regions of the Mediterranean.

Where to keep them

Sabina juniper (zones 4–7) is frost hardy but requires some protection from very hard frost, especially in wet winters. Keep the plants in a sunny position throughout the year.

Above: The new shoots of sabina juniper tend to be much longer than those of Chinese juniper cultivars. It can be quite a coarse grower.

How to look after them

REPOTTING: Repot every 3–4 years, in spring. Use free-draining compost of one part Akadama soil (or loam), one part humus (or peat) and two parts sharp sand. Or try equal parts of loam, leaf mould and sharp sand.

PRUNING AND PINCHING: Trim new shoots regularly. Some hobbyists prefer to prune rather than pinch but do not use the shears across the foliage when pruning, because this will leave brown tips on the foliage. It is much better to cut into the stem.

WIRING: This can be done at any time of year.

WATERING: Although sabina juniper does not need as much water as a deciduous tree, it still needs to be watered regularly, especially in the hot summer months. However, take care not to drown the plant.

FEEDING: In early spring, apply a high-nitrogen fertilizer. Feed with a general fertilizer every two months until autumn.

BE AWARE: Scale insects. can be a problem; treat them with an appropriate insecticide.

Juniperus sabina

Juniperus squamata

Squamata juniper

- *hardy evergreen*
- *needs frequent grooming to keep foliage looking fresh*
- *good tree for carving and driftwood effects*

This species, which originates from the Himalayas and western China, includes prostrate and erect shrubs and small trees. It produces prickly, blue needles and brown, flaky bark. Although any of the varieties and cultivars may be used for bonsai, *Juniperus squamata* 'Meyeri' is the most popular one for bonsai, on account of its upright habit. Squamata juniper needles require regular grooming, because the old needles turn brown and become very unsightly if left on the tree. Otherwise, this plant is easy to care for.

Above: The foliage of squamata juniper is steel-blue or grey in colour. Remove any dead needles regularly, in order to keep the tree looking fresh.

Where to keep them

This hardy evergreen (zones 5–8) likes full sun, but in summer give it some shade to enhance the needle colouring and prevent them from turning brown.

How to look after them

REPOTTING: Repot every 3–4 years, in late spring, using a gritty, open soil mix.
PRUNING AND PINCHING: Prune regularly in summer and remove old brown needles to keep the tree looking smart. Also keep trimming back the tips of new foliage.
WIRING: Squamata juniper may be wired at any time of the year. Remove old wires if you do not want them to mark the trunk.

WATERING: Water your bonsai regularly, starting with once a day in spring and early summer and increasing to twice daily in mid-summer. Towards the latter part of summer and into autumn, water once a day. In winter, keep the soil just moist. Never let the soil become waterlogged or dry out completely.

FEEDING: Feed in early spring and again in mid-summer with a general fertilizer to keep foliage blue and healthy. A late summer feed is also beneficial if foliage looks dull and tired.

BE AWARE: Squamata juniper is prone to juniper scale and red spider mites; treat with insecticide. If juniper blight occurs, cut out or burn infected branches or the entire plant. Remove old flaky bark in spring and again in autumn. The bark can also be brushed with a wire brush to enhance its reddish-brown colouring.

Juniperus squamata

Larix

Larch, Kara matsu

- *hardy*
- *deciduous*
- *easy to keep and train*
- *colourful foliage*

When larches are in leaf they resemble *Pinus* (see pages 78–89), despite being deciduous. In spring they have attractive, pale green foliage, which turns golden-yellow in autumn before it falls. The species used most often for bonsai are *Larix kaempferi* (Japanese larch), *L. decidua* (European larch) and *L. laricina* (American larch). In Europe, larches collected from the wild are popular and fetch high prices among enthusiasts. Larches are suitable for most bonsai styles, particularly forest and group plantings, and are available trained as bonsai from most bonsai nurseries.

Where to keep them

These hardy trees (zone 3) require no special protection in winter in temperate climates. In fact, they need cold temperatures to grow successfully. In central Japan, where summers are very warm and winters are mild and wet, larches tend to languish and their needles become coarse. This is probably why you do not see bonsai larches in Japan. Plants should be kept in full sun throughout the year.

Right: A larch tree produces cones when it is seven or eight years old. A mature specimen makes an interesting bonsai.

How to look after them

REPOTTING: Repot young larches every two years in mid-spring, and older ones every 3–4 years. Use a free-draining compost with one part leaf mould, one part loam and one part sharp sand.

PRUNING AND PINCHING: In spring, prune back any side branches that are too long, cutting just above a tuft of needles and taking care not to slice through the needles themselves. To keep the silhouette, trim throughout the growing season, remove shoots emerging from the trunk and pinch back the tips of new shoots developing on side branches.

WIRING: If necessary, apply wire in early summer and remove it in autumn. If you wire larches in autumn, the wires will have to stay on until the following autumn. Take care not to trap any needles under the wires.

WATERING: Water larch bonsai regularly, even in winter, so that the compost never dries out. Increase the amount of water given during summer. Make sure that the soil never becomes waterlogged. You can mist occasionally, but bear in mind that larches prefer a slightly dry atmosphere.

FEEDING: Apply a general fertilizer in spring and late summer. Do not overfeed larches, or the needles and branches will become coarse.

BE AWARE: Larch adelgids (aphid-like, sap-sucking pests) can be a problem on young shoots in early summer. They can be identified by a white, fluffy wax. Severe infestations lead to yellowing of the foliage. If a jet of water won't dislodge the pests, apply a systemic insecticide.

Larix decidua

Metasequoia glyptostroboides

Dawn redwood

- hardy
- deciduous
- fast growing
- easy to keep
- colourful foliage

This handsome tree, which was discovered in China as recently as 1941, can reach 40m (130ft) high in the wild. It has orange-brown bark and bright green foliage, which turns pinkish-brown, then golden-brown, in autumn. Dawn redwood is a good choice for bonsai and can be trained into most styles, especially the informal and formal upright styles. It is not used commercially for bonsai in Japan, but many North American and European nurseries have produced fine examples.

Where to keep them

Native to Hubei province in central China, dawn redwood (zones 4–5) is a hardy tree in temperate areas, yet it may need protection in areas where winter temperatures fall below -10°C (14°F). Keep in full sun during the growing season, but protect it from very hot sunshine, because the leaves may be in danger of burning.

How to look after them

REPOTTING: Repot every spring. Use a free-draining but moisture-retentive compost consisting of equal parts peat (or garden compost), sharp sand and loam. Dawn redwood is unusual among

Above: The foliage of the dawn redwood is similar to that of hemlock and yew, but softer and more delicate. In autumn, the colour is quite spectacular.

conifers in being able to tolerate waterlogged soil for short periods.

PRUNING AND PINCHING: New growth on dawn redwood is very soft, so allow shoots to harden before pruning. Use your fingers to pinch out the tips of new shoots as they emerge during the growing season; avoid scissors, as they can make the growing tips brown. Be careful, because young shoots can tear easily.

WIRING: Wire new shoots only when they have hardened slightly, or there is a danger of snapping them. Do not leave the wires on for longer than one growing season.

WATERING: Water regularly and generously throughout the growing season. In hot weather, you need to water two to three times a day. You can also stand the pot in a shallow tray of water to prevent it from drying out. In winter, keep the soil moist. Never allow the rootball to dry out.

FEEDING: In spring, apply a high-nitrogen feed and follow this with an application of a general fertilizer in late summer.

Metasequoia glyptostroboides

BE AWARE: Dawn redwood is largely trouble free in bonsai form, but it can be affected by mildew in very wet weather. Apply a suitable fungicide to treat this problem.

Picea jezoensis

Yezo spruce, Ezo matsu

- *hardy*
- *evergreen*
- *easy to keep*
- *challenging to train*
- *flaky bark*

This erect species has dark green needles in dense clusters, and grey-brown, flaky bark. It has long been a favourite among Japanese bonsai enthusiasts, who use Yezo spruce for both individual specimens and forest groups (if used as a single specimen, the trunk must be fairly thick to be convincing). Unfortunately, Yezo spruce is not as popular as it once was, and its importation into most countries outside Asia is extremely difficult, if not impossible. Some hobbyists, however, do grow it from seed or propagate from cuttings in early spring, which root easily.

Above: The compact growth habit of Yezo spruce makes it very suitable for bonsai, but the twigs and branches are difficult to wire without trapping the foliage.

Many Western enthusiasts have experimented with other varieties of ornamental spruce, such as *Picea abies* (Norway spruce), collected from the wild. These have proved just as successful bonsai subjects as Yezo spruce.

Where to keep them

Yezo spruce (zones 3–4) is a hardy tree from Manchuria, Japan and Korea, and can be kept outside all year round without any special protection. Shelter from prolonged cold spells of -10°C (14°F), and below, in a garage or shed. Keep it in full sun during summer.

How to look after them

REPOTTING: Repot Yezo spruce in spring every 3–4 years, but only when the tree is pot bound. If you repot too frequently the internodes will become too long. Use a free-draining mixture consisting of equal parts leaf mould, loam and sharp sand. Yezo spruce needs soil that is on the acid side of neutral; it will not thrive in alkaline conditions.

PRUNING AND PINCHING: Cut back the long branches in spring, leaving only a few tufts of needles. Cut immediately above a tuft of needles, taking care not to slice through the needles themselves. Throughout the growing season, pinch out the tips of new shoots, with your fingers. This will keep the foliage pads compact and prevent the tree from becoming leggy.

WIRING: Wire Yezo spruce in late autumn or early winter, and leave the wire in place for a year. Take special care not to trap needles under the wire.

WATERING: Water Yezo spruce regularly throughout the year, giving it more water during the dry summer months. Allow the surface of the soil to dry slightly between waterings, because this species does not survive in waterlogged soil.

FEEDING: Apply a high-nitrogen fertilizer in early spring. In late summer, feed with a general fertilizer.

BE AWARE: Aphids and red spider mites can cluster on new shoots. If they cannot be removed with a jet of water, apply a systemic insecticide. Treat sap-sucking adelgids with a systemic insecticide.

Picea jezoensis

Pinus mugo

Dwarf mountain pine, Swiss mountain pine

- *hardy*
- *evergreen*
- *easy to keep*
- *scaly, grey bark*
- *good driftwood*

Dwarf mountain pine is a sturdy, compact tree with short branches, a gnarled trunk with scaly, grey bark, and dark green needles borne in pairs. It can be used for any bonsai style, although gnarled specimens are best trained in the driftwood style, and young plants look good as informal upright, cascade or windswept bonsai. Stock suitable for smaller bonsai can be quite easily purchased from nurseries and garden centres. However, it is the larger, older trees that grow wild in mountainous areas which attract many hobbyists. Prior written permission should always be obtained from the owner before removing such material.

Above: The needles of dwarf mountain pines are easy to recognize – being twisted and encased in a waxy sheath at the base of the cluster.

Wild bonsai specimens are often 80 or more years old, and they make spectacular specimen bonsai with thick, gnarled trunks and masses of deadwood in the form of jins and sharis (see page 33).

Where to keep them

This central European species (zone 2) is fully hardy in temperate areas. Plants do not normally require any special protection in winter, although it might be worth giving an expensive specimen some protection if temperatures fall below -5°C (23°F). Place dwarf mountain pine in full sun in the growing season.

How to look after them

REPOTTING: Once every 5–8 years is quite sufficient, and as long as the tree appears to be healthy there is no need to repot. When it is necessary, repot in mid-spring and use free-draining compost consisting of equal parts leaf mould, loam and sharp sand. Dwarf mountain pine is not fussy about soil, although it tends to be short-lived in chalky conditions.

PRUNING AND PINCHING: Prune away unwanted branches any time from spring to autumn. Cut just above a cluster of needles. Sealing is not required after pruning, because pines exude resin, which acts as a cut paste. Pinch out the candles as they emerge in late spring. In a cluster of three or five candles, remove one or two of the strongest ones.

WIRING: Wire branches at any time of the year, except when new shoots are growing. Take care not to trap needles under the wire. The wires can be left on for 1–2 years.

WATERING: Water regularly, with more water given in summer. In winter, keep the compost moist.

FEEDING: Apply a general fertilizer in spring and autumn, but do not feed between mid- and late summer. Overfeeding will encourage coarse growth and thickening of the branches.

BE AWARE: Pine adelgids (sap-sucking insects) can be a problem from mid- to late spring. Spraying in late spring is often ineffective, and the best treatment is to spray the overwintering nymphs with an insecticide in late winter.

Pinus mugo

OUTDOOR CONIFEROUS BONSAI

Pinus parviflora

Japanese white pine, Five needle pine, Goyo matsu

- *hardy*
- *evergreen*
- *easy to keep*
- *elegant shape*
- *scaly, grey bark*

Japanese white pine is one of the most popular evergreen conifers for bonsai and has been used for centuries in both China and Japan. It is an elegant, upright tree with deeply fissured, greyish bark. Soft needles, borne in tufts of five, are green-blue on the outer surface and blue-white on the inner. Japanese white pine is suitable for different single-tree styles of bonsai, most popularly the informal upright style. Wild-collected specimens are extremely valuable, and most of the major exhibition trees in Japan are from this source.

Elegant examples of Japanese white pine are greatly sought after, and most bonsai nurseries stock bonsai from this species. Two recent cultivars, *Pinus parviflora* 'Zui-sho' and *P.p.* 'Kokonoe', have particularly small, compact needles.

When Japanese white pine is grown commercially in Japan for bonsai, plants are normally grafted on to rootstock of *P. thunbergii* (see pages 88–9), which gives a strong, vigorous tree. When it is grown on its own roots, Japanese white

pine is less vigorous and usually has a slightly yellow tinge.

Above: The flowers and candles of the Japanese white pine develop in late spring. Allow the flowers to blossom, but do not encourage the cones to set.

Where to keep them

Japanese white pine (zone 5) comes from the mountains of central and southern Japan and is hardy in most temperate areas. In areas where temperatures fall below -3°C (27°F), protect in an unheated shed or greenhouse. It can also be grown in Mediterranean areas. In the growing season, place in full sun.

How to look after them

REPOTTING: Small bonsai should be repotted in early spring every 3–4 years, and larger specimens every 5–6 years.

Never remove more than a quarter of the old soil, and use a free-draining mix consisting of equal parts leaf mould, loam and sharp sand. Or try equal parts of Akadama soil and sharp sand.

PRUNING AND PINCHING: Prune back the longest branches in mid-autumn, cutting above a cluster of needles. Sealing is not required, because pines exude resin, which acts as a cut paste. Pinch out the new candles with your fingers in late spring. In a cluster of three or five candles, remove one or two of the strongest ones.

WIRING: Wire in spring and leave the wires in place until the branches have set, unless they begin to bite into the bark.

WATERING: Water regularly in the growing season, giving more water in summer. In winter, keep the compost moist, but never waterlogged. Allow the surface of the compost to dry slightly between waterings.

FEEDING: Apply small quantities of rapeseed fertilizer in the growing season. Do not overfeed.

BE AWARE: Spray adelgids with an appropriate insecticide.

Pinus parviflora

Pinus ponderosa

Ponderosa pine, Western yellow pine, Blackjack pine

- hardy, evergreen American pine
- not often seen outside the USA
- enormous potential as bonsai material

Ponderosa pine is found mainly in western areas of North America. It is one of the most common pines in this region and is highly suitable for bonsai. It has distinctive, dark to red-brown bark and long needles. The species has needles in clusters of three, while some subspecies bear them in twos, threes, fours or even fives. It is easy to grow from seed, and good specimens are usually collected from the wild.

Above: The stiff, dark green needles of ponderosa pine resemble those of Japanese black pine and *Pinus mugo* (dwarf mountain pine).

Where to keep them

This very hardy tree (zones 3–7) tolerates hard frost as well as drought and harsh conditions. Grow in full sun and keep in an open area for good air circulation. It may need some shade in very hot summers.

How to look after them

REPOTTING: Repot every 4–5 years, in late spring, using a mix of two parts grit and one part loam. Keep root removal to a minimum, because ponderosa pine does not like too much root cut off when being repotted.

PRUNING AND PINCHING: Remove or pinch out the new candles from mid- to late spring, to encourage bud back and denser growth. The older needles can be cut short in late summer, to allow light to penetrate the branches and encourage bud formation.

WIRING: Wire any time of the year. Ponderosa pine takes to wiring well.

WATERING: Be sparing with watering because ponderosa pine likes dry conditions. During very hot spells, more water may needed to keep the roots cool. Excessive watering will result in long needles, so a careful balance needs to be struck.

FEEDING: Feed a half-strength general fertilizer in spring. Excessive fertilizer will result in long needles.

BE AWARE: Prone to mildew if overwatered. Treat with fungicide.

Pinus ponderosa

Pinus radiata

Monterey pine

- *evergreen conifer originally from California*
- *easy to grow from seed*
- *now available in most countries – though not as bonsai*
- *simple to make into bonsai from ordinary nursery material*

The Monterey pine is a native of the Californian coast but since the 20th century has been planted in most Mediterranean and subtropical countries as a valuable commercial timber tree. As it is such a prolific grower, Monterey pine is the most widely planted pine in the world. Each tuft bears two (sometimes three) needles, and it has deep-fissured bark. It makes excellent bonsai.

Where to keep them

Monterey pine (zones 8– 10) likes a mild climate and plenty of moisture, but can tolerate only a slight frost, so needs protection in winter. Keep in full sun, but in very hot weather provide some shade during the afternoon.

How to look after them

REPOTTING: Do this in late spring using very open, free-draining compost consisting of equal parts sand and loam. Most pines do not need to be repotted

Left: The needles of Monterey pine are long and bright green, borne in clusters of two or three. Needle length does reduce when the bonsai is kept slightly pot bound.

more than once every 3–5 years. Older, larger specimens can be left even longer before repotting. Do not remove too much root when repotting Monterey pine – 10–20 per cent is sufficient.

PRUNING AND PINCHING: Prune in late summer. Pinch out candles in early summer to encourage back budding.

WIRING: Wire at any time.

WATERING: As this is a coastal pine from California, Monterey pine enjoys moist air and mild sea breezes. Do not let the soil dry out. It likes more water than other pine species.

FEEDING: Apply a general fertilizer in spring, but sparingly, as heavy feeding encourages coarse and vigorous growth.

BE AWARE: Look out for aphids and adelgids, and treat any infestation with an appropriate insecticide, or just wash off the pests with jets of water.

Pinus radiata

Pinus sylvestris

Scots pine

- *hardy*
- *evergreen*
- *easy to grow*
- *upright growth*
- *flaky bark*

Scots pine has an upright habit with a spreading crown and flaky, red-brown or orange bark. The needles, which may be blue-green or yellow-green, are borne in pairs. This tree makes a delightful bonsai, and enthusiasts have created some beautiful specimens. Unfortunately, Scots pine bonsai are not widely available, but examples are worth seeking out, and some bonsai nurseries occasionally stock semi-trained, collected material.

Scots pine tends to be a leggy plant, so is suitable for the literati style, which features a bare, slender trunk. The dwarf forms of Scots pine, such as *P. sylvestris* 'Beuvronensis', are more compact and, therefore, more suitable for styles such as the informal upright, slanting, windswept and cascade.

Where to keep them

Scots pine (zone 3) is a hardy plant found originally throughout Europe and in temperate Asia. It requires no special winter protection, and it should be kept in full sun throughout the growing season.

How to look after them

REPOTTING: In mid-spring, repot young Scots pine every 3–4 years and larger and older specimens every 5–6 years or so. Use free-draining compost consisting of equal parts leaf mould, loam and sharp sand.

Left: These full-sized needles of Scots pine display the lovely, greyish-blue colouring of a healthy and vigorous tree.

PRUNING AND PINCHING: Prune Scots pine between summer and late autumn, removing any unwanted shoots or branches, preferably at a leaf or stem junction. Take care not to cut through any of the needles, because they will turn brown. Sealing the cuts is not required after pruning, as pines exude resin, which acts as a cut paste. Pinch out the candles, with your fingers, as the needles lengthen in late spring. In a cluster of three or five candles, remove one or two of the strongest ones.

WIRING: Wire Scots pine in autumn and winter, taking care not to trap needles under the wire. Remove the wires in late summer to early autumn, when the branches thicken.

WATERING: Water regularly throughout the growing season, giving more water in summer. Keep the compost moist in winter, but never allow it to become waterlogged. The surface of the compost should be allowed to dry slightly between waterings.

FEEDING: Apply a moderate amount of rapeseed fertilizer in mid-summer. Overfeeding Scots pines will encourage the needles to grow long and the branches to thicken prematurely.

BE AWARE: Like other pines, Scots pine is susceptible to adelgids. These pests appear mainly in spring and summer; spray with an appropriate insecticide to control them. Scots pine sheds its old needles in autumn. If you pick off all the old needles with your fingers, the tree will soon regain its healthy appearance.

Pinus sylvestris

87

Pinus thunbergii

Japanese black pine, Kuro matsu

- *hardy*
- *evergreen*
- *easy to grow*
- *upright growth*
- *scaly, black bark*

Japanese black pine and *P. thunbergii* var. *corticosa* (cork-bark Japanese black pine) have always been popular in Japan as both garden trees and bonsai. They have an upright habit, stiff, dark green needles borne in pairs, and dark, fissured bark that gives the trunks an imposing, characterful appearance and increases their popularity. Depending on a tree's age, it will be suitable for bonsai styles such as informal upright, cascade and driftwood.

It is almost impossible to import Japanese black pine from Japan. Those that are sold are illegal imports. Some European, North American and Australian bonsai nurseries grow Japanese black pine from seed, but they do not achieve the same quality as Japanese examples.

Where to keep them

Japanese black pine (zones 5–6) is native to north-eastern China, Japan and Korea, and it is hardy in most temperate areas. When winter temperatures are likely to fall below -5°C (23°F) for prolonged periods, protect trees in a frost-free shed or greenhouse. During the growing season, place in full sun.

How to look after them

REPOTTING: Repot young trees in late spring every 3–4 years; larger specimens

Left: Japanese black pine has stiff, upright, dark green needles and crusty, black bark that gives it a very rugged appearance.

need repotting every 5–6 years. Use free-draining compost consisting of equal parts leaf mould, loam and sharp sand. Or try two parts of Akadama soil and one part grit (or sharp sand).

Pinus thunbergii

PRUNING AND PINCHING: Prune specimens of Japanese black pine between summer and late autumn, removing any unwanted shoots or branches, preferably at a stem or leaf junction. Take care not to cut through any needles. Sealing is not required. Pinch out the new candles with your fingers in late spring. In a cluster of three or five candles, remove one or two of the strongest ones.

WIRING: Wire in autumn or winter, removing the wire before the branches thicken by the following late summer.

WATERING: Water regularly throughout the growing season, giving more water during summer. Keep the compost moist in winter, but never allow it to become waterlogged. The surface of the compost should be allowed to dry slightly between waterings.

FEEDING: Apply a general fertilizer in mid-spring or early summer. Too much fertilizer will lead to coarse growth, with long needles and thick branches.

BE AWARE: Adelgids can be a problem in spring. The best treatment is to spray the overwintering nymphs with an appropriate insecticide in late winter. Pick off caterpillars by hand as soon as they are noticed.

89

Pseudolarix amabilis

Golden larch, Chinese larch, False larch

- *easy to grow*
- *may need winter protection from hard frost*
- *easy to germinate from seed*
- *can be used for any style of bonsai*

Golden larch originates from southern China. It has beautiful, lime-green foliage during spring, which turns golden-yellow in summer and may even show a hint of orange in autumn. It is a deciduous conifer like its larch counterparts *Larix decidua* and *L. kaempferi* (see pages 72–3).

Where to keep them

Although golden larch (zones 5–9) originates from southern China, it is quite hardy in mild temperate climates but may need protection in colder regions. It grows well in Mediterranean regions and may also be cultivated in subtropical areas. Golden larch is not as vigorous as *Larix decidua* and *L. kaempferi*. Place in full sun during the growing season, but it may need protection from hard frosts in cool-temperate regions.

Left: Golden larch has distinctive coloured foliage quite unlike that of other larches. The needle-shaped leaves start off lime-green or pale yellow in spring, and in autumn they turn to pure gold or russet-brown.

How to look after them

REPOTTING:
Repot every 2–3
years, in spring,
using compost
consisting of
equal parts
of peat, loam
and sand

**PRUNING AND
PINCHING:** Prune
during the growing
season to keep the
tree tidy, although it is
not a fast grower.

WIRING: Trunk and branches can
be wired at any time of the year.

WATERING: Golden larch needs
regular watering in summer.
Foliage will shrivel if this is not done.

FEEDING: A light feed during early
spring is usually sufficient to keep the
tree healthy.

BE AWARE: Golden larch is not prone
to any disease or pests.

Pseudolarix amabilis

Sequoia sempervirens
Coastal redwood

- *hardy evergreen*
- *easy to grow*
- *best for temperate regions*
- *collected specimens are best*

Coastal redwood is greatly treasured by any bonsai collector. This evergreen tree, which is one of the tallest trees in nature, is certainly one of the US's iconic trees. It has been used there for bonsai ever since the hobby started after the Second World War. It makes stunning and impressive bonsai, especially trees with massive trunks. Coastal redwood is fairly easy to keep and can readily be propagated from seeds or cuttings. Good specimens are not usually available from commercial nurseries.

Where to keep them

Coastal redwood (zones 7–9) has been successfully grown outside North America, in areas such as Europe, New Zealand, Argentina and South Africa. It needs some winter protection from very cold temperatures of -10°C (14°F). This tree likes full sun, although in very hot summers some shade is beneficial.

How to look after them

REPOTTING: Repot coastal redwood every 2–3 years, from mid- to late

Left: The shoots of coastal redwood droop slightly, but on the short branches of a bonsai this is not a problem. Its foliage is similar to that of yew.

spring. Some Californian growers repot throughout the year, however. Use a standard mix of equal parts of peat, loam and sand.

PRUNING AND PINCHING: As coastal redwood is a fast grower, frequent pruning and pinching are necessary.

WIRING: Wire young shoots and branches when they have just hardened. This can be done at any time of the year.

WATERING: Give lots of water during the growing season. They can even be stood in water during summer. Keep the soil just damp in winter.

FEEDING: Feed with a general fertilizer from spring to late summer.

BE AWARE: Bark beetles can be a problem; treat with an appropriate insecticide. Root rot can sometimes be troublesome, so watch out for leaf wilt and any other unusual symptoms.

Sequoia sempervirens

Sequoiadendron giganteum

Wellingtonia, Californian redwood, Giant redwood

- *hardy evergreen*
- *fast growing*
- *challenging subject*
- *impressive when grown well*

Wellingtonia is a stately tree with lovely, corky, reddish-brown bark and green foliage. A very vigorous grower, it takes a lot of effort to keep it small when grown as a bonsai, so hobbyists find it a very challenging tree. It is not available as a commercial bonsai although the plants themselves can be sourced from nurseries and garden centres.

Above: Wellingtonia has awl-shaped leaves, which are mid- to deep green in colour.

Where to keep them

Wellingtonia (zones 6–9) is a hardy tree suitable for temperate and Mediterranean climates. It should be kept in full sun during the growing season. It may need winter protection to prevent branch die-back.

How to look after them

REPOTTING: This vigorous grower needs to be repotted every couple of years. As with most temperate- and Mediterranean-zone trees, spring is the best time to do this. Use compost consisting of equal parts peat, sharp sand and loam.

PRUNING AND PINCHING: Wellngtonia produces new shoots readily, while older branches have a habit of dying back. Prune with scissors, because pinching may be difficult.

WIRING: Wire branches regularly, as their natural tendency is to grow upwards. Remove wires in winter, because the cold can damage any wired branches.

WATERING: Wellingtonia needs moderate but regular watering during the growing season.

FEEDING: Feed with a general fertilizer in early spring to encourage new growth and keep the foliage green.

BE AWARE: Branch die-back is a problem. If branches die, do not despair because new shoots will develop into branches fairly quickly.

Sequoiadendron giganteum

Taxodium distichum

Swamp cypress, Bald cypress, Deciduous cypress

- *very easy species to grow and keep*
- *suitable for temperate to tropical climates*
- *need lots of water*
- *impressive bonsai with massive trunks*

This stately, deciduous tree has a straight strong-buttressed trunk covered in beautiful, red bark. Its leaves are pale green in spring and turn reddish brown in autumn. Swamp cypress is very popular as bonsai in the US, where it is often collected from wild swampy areas in Florida and Louisiana. It is also a popular species for bonsai in China.

Where to keep them

Swamp cypress (zones 5–10) is a native of the southern US and tolerates frost up to -5°C (23°F), but not harder ones. Therefore, protect from severe frost in cold winters. Keep in full sun during the growing season.

How to look after them

REPOTTING: In zones 5–10, bonsai growers prefer to repot in the dormant season. In other regions, repotting in spring may be better. Do this every year, using loam-based compost.

Left: Swamp cypress produces soft, delicate foliage, which is light green in spring and turns golden-brown in autumn.

Taxodium distichum

PRUNING AND PINCHING: Prune frequently, because swamp cypress is vigorous. It can be defoliated in mid-summer in tropical areas (see page 30).

WIRING: Wire during the growing season or after defoliating in summer. The wires can be left on for a year or until the branches have set.

WATERING: As swamp cypress prefers swampy ground, it needs copious amounts of water when it is grown as a bonsai plant. As with *Salix* (see pages 160–1), it can also be stood in water during the summer months. After defoliating in the summer, you can safely reduce the watering slightly.

FEEDING: Feed with a general fertilizer in spring. If you defoliate in summer (see page 30), feed again once the leaves emerge after defoliation.

BE AWARE: Aphids and red spider mites are attracted to this species. Treat them with a suitable insecticide or wash off these pests with a jet of water. Check for root aphids at regular intervals; use insecticide to control them.

Taxus

Yew

- hardy
- evergreen
- easy to train
- deep green foliage
- good driftwood

In recent years, *Taxus baccata* (common yew, English yew) and *T. cuspidata* (Japanese yew, Ichi) have become popular as bonsai. These traditional garden trees have only recently caught the imagination of bonsai enthusiasts. They are suitable for most styles, but particularly for bonsai where there is lots of driftwood. Exquisite jins and sharis (see page 33) can be created from the superfluous branches. Yew has lovely, dark green foliage, and new shoots grow easily from old wood. Ready-trained plants can be found in most bonsai nurseries, and nursery material is easy to train into bonsai.

Where to keep them

Common yew (zones 4–5) is native to Europe, east into Iran and north Africa, while Japanese yew (zones 4–5) is native in north-east China and Japan. Both species are hardy in temperate areas, but in areas that experience prolonged temperatures below -5°C (23°F) move plants to a frost-free greenhouse or shed. Place both species in full sun in summer.

How to look after them

REPOTTING: Repot young yews in spring every 2–3 years; and older specimens

Above: Yew produces lovely red berries with poisonous seeds. The foliage of Japanese yew (shown here) grows radially, unlike the flat leaves of common yew.

every 3–4 years. Use a free-draining
compost of two parts Akadama soil
(or loam), one part peat (or garden
compost) and one part sharp sand.
Yews are tolerant of most soil types,
including acid and chalky soils.

PRUNING AND PINCHING: Prune
yews in spring or autumn, cutting
the secondary shoots back above a
tuft of needles and taking care not to
slice through the needles. Pinch out the
growing tips of young shoots with your
fingers between spring and autumn.

WIRING: Wire from early autumn to early
spring, but avoid wiring soft branches.
Do not trap needles under the wire.
Leave wires on until the branch sets;
this takes 1–5 years, depending on the
thickness and age of the branch.

WATERING: Water regularly throughout
the growing season, giving more water
in summer. Although the soil should
never be allowed to dry out completely
in winter, do not allow it to become
too wet, because the combination of
waterlogged soil and frost can damage
yew roots.

FEEDING: Apply a general fertilizer to
yews in spring and early autumn. If the

Taxus cuspidata

leaves look yellow in spring, give the
plants a high-nitrogen feed.

BE AWARE: Scale insects can be a
problem on old leaves, while young
leaves are sometimes attacked by aphids.
Try removing the aphids by jetting them
with bursts of water. Otherwise, apply
a systemic insecticide. Winter frosts
sometimes turn yew foliage reddish-
brown, but be assured that it will revert
to green in the spring.

Thuja occidentalis

Eastern white cedar

- *hardy evergreen*
- *easy to keep*
- *likes a cool-temperate climate*
- *hobbyist's tree*
- *not often seen in commercial bonsai nurseries*

Eastern white cedar is one of the cypresses native to north-eastern US and the south-eastern states of Canada. It is used extensively as an ornamental tree because it bears lovely foliage and interesting, reddish-brown bark. The foliage, which is in the form of flat fronds, is not dissimilar to that of *Chamaecyparis obtusa* (see page 48). It is easy to propagate from seeds or cuttings, and can be trained into bonsai quite readily. Any gnarled, old specimen bonsai are usually trees collected from the wild, where harsh growing conditions has given them immense character. Eastern white cedar is very much an amateur grower's species.

Where to keep them

This very hardy species (zones 1– 10) benefits from some winter protection to keep its leaves green, because hard frosts tend to turn them reddish brown. Place in full sun during summer.

Left: The cones of eastern white cedar resemble those of other cypresses, including Hinoki cypress. The foliage fronds too are very similar. Both foliage and cones have a lovely resinous fragrance when crushed.

How to look after them

REPOTTING: Repot every 2– 3 years, in late spring. Use moderately free-draining soil of equal parts loam and grit.

PRUNING AND PINCHING: Finger pinch at regular intervals to keep foliage dense, and prune with shears at least twice a year. Do not allow foliage to grow too long, as it will be difficult to get it dense again.

WIRING: The flat foliage fronds of Eastern white cedar make wiring difficult, but they can be wired. Summer wiring is best.

WATERING: Eastern white cedar requires a lot of water in the growing season. Water sparingly in winter.

FEEDING: Feed with a high-nitrogen fertilizer in spring, and with a low-nitrogen one in late summer.

BE AWARE: Old foliage will shed in autumn, so do not panic. Eastern white cedar can be affected by scale insects and leaf miners. Spray with any insecticide to control such pests.

Thuja occidentalis

Tsuga

Hemlock

- hardy
- evergreen
- easy to keep
- delicate foliage
- dark, scaly bark
- popular with amateurs

These handsome, hardy conifers make good bonsai. Suitable species include *Tsuga canadensis* (eastern hemlock), *T. diversifolia* (northern Japanese hemlock), *T. heterophylla* (western hemlock) and *T. sieboldii* (southern Japanese hemlock). Hemlocks have an upright, conical habit and dark green leaves, which are similar to those of *Taxus* (see pages 98–9) but more refined. The purplish-brown, fissured bark flakes attractively. The most commonly available species is eastern hemlock, which can be used for most styles.

Above: Hemlocks bear a striking resemblance to yews. Pictured here are the needles of western hemlock.

Where to keep them

Originating in western North America, eastern hemlock (zones 2–4) is hardy. It needs special protection in winter only during prolonged periods of freezing weather, when plants should be moved to a frost-free shed or greenhouse. In summer, keep plants in full sun, although they appreciate some shade from direct sunshine at the height of summer.

How to look after them

REPOTTING: Repot hemlocks in spring every 3–5 years. Use a moisture-retentive, free-draining compost consisting of equal parts peat (or garden compost), loam and sharp sand. They prefer soil on the acid side of neutral.

PRUNING AND PINCHING: Prune hemlocks in spring or autumn, cutting back branches above a tuft of needles and taking care not to slice through any needles. Pinch out the growing tips of young shoots with your fingers as they emerge between spring and autumn.

WIRING: Wiring should be done between early autumn and early spring, but avoid wiring soft, non-woody branches. The twigs tend to be very slender, so wiring should be delicate and precise. Use copper wire for exhibition trees, and take care to avoid trapping foliage under the wire. The wire can be left on for 2–3 years, until it starts to bite into the bark. Wiring can be kept to a minimum with small-needled varieties if the new shoots are trimmed regularly and pruned hard back to old wood – in fact some hobbyists do not wire at all.

WATERING: Water regularly throughout the growing season, giving more water in summer. If a tree has not been repotted for several years, make sure the rootball is thoroughly soaked when you water. Keep the compost moist in winter.

FEEDING: Apply a high-nitrogen fertilizer in spring. Afterwards, change to a low-nitrogen feed and apply once a month until late summer. Do not feed these plants during winter.

BE AWARE: Scale insects can sometimes be a problem on hemlock trees; treat them with a systemic insecticide.

Tsuga diversifolia

Outdoor broad-leaved BONSAI

Introduction

Broad-leaved bonsai are usually deciduous species, which are integral to the natural landscape of the world's temperate regions and provide an endless cycle of rich imagery throughout the year. Their bright, fresh foliage emerges in spring and, as the leaves mature, changes to darker shades of green. When autumn arrives, the trees assume colourful hues. Even in winter, when they have shed their leaves, the fine tracery of branches and twigs has a sublime beauty.

Care of broad-leaved bonsai

Broad-leaved bonsai are, in general, deciduous, with a handful of exceptions such as semi-evergreen *Lonicera nitida* (see pages 148–9) and evergreen *Quercus suber* (see pages 158–9). Deciduous bonsai go through the seasons in exactly the same way as their fully grown counterparts in the open countryside and in our gardens. Regular pinching is key to achieving smaller-sized leaves and a fine framework of branches. However, the most onerous part of keeping all deciduous bonsai is watering. (See pages 26–41 for details on looking after broad-leaved and other bonsai.)

Left: Japanese maple *Acer palmatum* in its autumn colour grown in the semi-cascade style.

Above: Plants with small leaves, such as hedging honeysuckle, are the right scale to make ideal bonsai subjects.

Above: Maples are among the most popular bonsai subjects. They offer great variety of leaf shape and colour and interesting bark.

Broad-leaved species

The most popular deciduous plants used for bonsai are small trees, such as cultivars of *Acer palmatum* (see pages 112–17). Larger trees and those with large leaves can be used, too. Both *Aesculus hippocastanum* (see pages 118–19) and *Quercus robur* (see pages 156–7) are naturally large trees, and they make exquisite bonsai. The challenge and fascination of bonsai lies in achieving the miniaturization of such species through standard bonsai cultivation techniques. In fact, if treated sympathetically, any tree or shrub can be made into a fine bonsai.

Acer palmatum and *A. buergerianum* (see pages 108–9) are probably the most widely cultivated deciduous bonsai in Japan. There are so many cultivars, offering such a wide range of foliage colour, shape and habit of growth, that many bonsai enthusiasts specialize in growing maples and nothing else. Most are hardy and can withstand fairly low winter temperatures, and they also require relatively little care, apart from regular pinching and pruning in summer. Most shaping is achieved through pruning, so wiring can be kept to a minimum.

Other popular deciduous genera that are used for easy-to-keep bonsai are *Carpinus* (see pages 126–31), *Fagus* (see pages 134–5), *Salix* (see pages 160–1) and *Ulmus* (see pages 164–7).

107

Acer buergerianum

Trident maple, Three-toothed maple, Kaede

- *hardy*
- *deciduous*
- *easy to train*
- *good leaf shape*
- *vivid autumn colour*

This popular maple for bonsai is a fast-growing plant, which will rapidly produce a thick trunk with lots of character. The attractive leaves turn pink in autumn, and in winter the fine branch and twig structure gives the trees an elegant outline. Trident maple, which is often grown in the root-over-rock style, is a firm favourite with all bonsai enthusiasts. Young plants are easy to train and are widely available from bonsai nurseries.

Where to keep them

Although trident maple (zone 6), which is native to eastern China, Korea and Japan, is hardy, like other maples it requires some protection in areas where winter temperatures fall below -3°C (27°F). It prefers full sun in the growing season, but it also benefits from partial shade when temperatures exceed 27°C (80°F), because strong direct sunshine will scorch its leaves.

How to look after them

REPOTTING: Repot trident maple every other year, during early spring, when

the buds are about to break. But check the rootball first: if the plant is not pot

Above: The new growth of trident maple is bronze in colour. Like the foliage of most deciduous trees, the leaves of this species will change colour with the seasons.

bound, there is no need to repot. The leaves will become smaller if plants are kept slightly pot bound. Take care not to remove more than one-third of the roots when you are repotting. Repot into Akadama soil or a reputable commercial bonsai compost.

PRUNING AND PINCHING: Any major pruning is best done in summer, when the trees are growing vigorously and cuts heal quickly. Branches can be cut back even as far as the main trunk. To keep the tree in good shape, start pinching out the growing tips of new shoots in spring, when two or three leaves have formed, continuing to do so throughout the growing season.

WIRING: Wire in spring. Wire marks on maples are unsightly, so you may need to protect the stems with raffia. Shaping with guy wires (see page 33) and by pinching and pruning helps to avoid marking. Do not leave the wires on for more than six months, and remove them as soon as they bite into the bark.

WATERING: Never allow trident maple to dry out completely during the growing season; nor should you overwater. Wait until the compost surface is slightly dry before watering. In spring and summer you might have to water twice a day. In winter, make sure that the compost remains just moist; do not overwater.

FEEDING: Start with a high-nitrogen fertilizer in spring and change to a monthly application of a low-nitrogen fertilizer in late summer. Do not feed in winter, when the tree is not growing.

BE AWARE: Aphids, scale insects and mites are the main pests. If you cannot pick off all of these pests by hand, apply a systemic insecticide.

Acer buergerianum

Acer campestre

Field maple, Hedge maple

- *hardy*
- *deciduous*
- *easy to train*
- *good leaf shape*
- *vivid autumn colour*

This tree, which is used extensively for hedging in Europe, has the palmate leaves typical of other maples. They are dark green, turning clear yellow or orange in autumn, before they fall. Field maple's habit is similar to that of *Acer buergerianum* (see pages 108–9), and it can be used for most styles of bonsai. Although field maple is widely available, commercially grown bonsai are not often found. It is is sold quite cheaply as hedging material and will thicken rapidly if planted in the ground and left to grow for a couple of years. Field maple is certainly one of the easiest trees to train into bonsai.

Where to keep them

Field maple (zone 5) comes from Europe, North Africa and south-western Asia, and it is completely hardy. Keep plants in full sun during the growing season to ensure that the leaves colour well. It does not require protection in winter.

How to look after them

REPOTTING: Repot field maple every 2–3 years, but only if the roots are very compacted or pot bound. The best time to do this is in late winter or early spring, when the new buds are just beginning to show. Bear in mind that the leaves will become smaller if plants

Left: The leaves of field maple will reduce dramatically in size when the tree is confined in a pot as a bonsai, especially if it is a little pot bound.

are kept slightly pot bound. Do not remove more than one-third of the root when repotting. Use Akadama soil or a reputable commercial bonsai compost.

PRUNING AND PINCHING: Prune back old growth on field maple during spring or summer. This species makes a fast-growing bonsai, so you can cut back as hard as necessary. To keep your tree in good shape, begin to pinch out the growing tips of any new shoots in spring, as soon as two or three leaves have formed, continuing to do this task throughout the growing season.

WIRING: Spring is the best time for wiring. Wire marks on maples are unsightly, so you may need to protect the stems with raffia. Shaping with guy wires (see page 33) and using pinching and pruning techniques helps to avoid unsightly marking. Do not leave the wires on for more than six months, and remove wires as soon as they begin to bite into the bark.

WATERING: Water field maple copiously from spring until autumn. It may need

Acer campestre

watering twice a day in summer. Keep the soil just moist in winter.

FEEDING: Apply a general fertilizer about once a month from spring until late summer.

BE AWARE: Like all maples, field maple is often infested with aphids, mites and scale insects. Apply a systemic insecticide, following the rate recommended by the manufacturer, if there are too many pests to pick off by hand.

Acer palmatum

Japanese maple, Mountain maple, Yamamomiji

- *hardy*
- *deciduous*
- *easy to train*
- *good leaf shape*
- *elegant*
- *vivid colours*

Japanese maple is one of the most popular deciduous species for bonsai. It is a flamboyant, showy tree, which is fairly easy to keep and which will give endless years of pleasure. The species is often called mountain maple or yamamomiji, to distinguish it from the many named cultivars that are available (see pages 114–17). In early spring, the new leaves emerge a pale green or bronze colour; they turn slightly darker in summer and finally flame-red in autumn. The delicate form of Japanese maple is suitable for most bonsai styles except windswept and driftwood.

Where to keep them

The species (zones 5–8), which originates in China, Korea and Japan, is hardy in cool-temperate areas. It does not do well in Mediterranean or tropical areas and should not be kept indoors, except for a day or two. Japanese maple will withstand winter temperatures as low as -10°C (14°F), but only for brief periods. If prolonged freezing conditions are forecast, protect in an unheated greenhouse or shed. It can be kept in full sun throughout summer, and will

Above: This Japanese maple is grown in the root-over-rock style. The foliage is about to reach the spectacular peak of its autumn display.

produce better autumn colours than if grown in shade. However, provide protection from fierce sunlight in mid-summer so that the foliage does not become scorched.

How to look after them

REPOTTING: Repot every 2–3 years, but only if the roots are pot bound. Early spring is the best time to do this, when new buds are just beginning to show. Use Akadama of the appropriate size or a compost that has some Akadama mixed in it. Maple leaves are smaller if the tree is kept slightly pot bound.

PRUNING AND PINCHING: Prune back the first flush of growth in early summer, and again in mid-summer. Pinching out new growth throughout the growing season will create a good framework.

WIRING: Wire in spring. Do not leave wire on for more than six months. Remove wires as soon as they begin to bite into the bark. Shaping with guy wires (see page 33) is sometimes preferable to wiring.

WATERING: Japanese maple needs a lot of water. Never let the soil dry out completely.

FEEDING: Use a high-nitrogen fertilizer during spring, and a low-nitrogen one in late summer.

BE AWARE: Aphids and scale insects love new leaves. Spray with insecticide or just wash off the insects with a jet of water.

Acer palmatum

Acer palmatum cultivars

Japanese maple varieties 1

- *hardy*
- *deciduous*
- *easy to train*
- *attractive leaf shape*
- *vivid colours*

Acer palmatum 'Beni-chidori', *A.p.* 'Deshōjō', *A.p.* 'Seigai' and *A.p.* 'Shishio' are mostly grown for their stunning, spring foliage colouring. The leaves of different Japanese maple cultivars all vary slightly in shape and colour, ranging from soft pink to fiery red. The autumn tints, however, are not as spectacular as those of the species. These trees are suitable for most styles except windswept and driftwood.

'BENI-CHIDORI': Although similar to 'Deshōjō', 'Beni-chidori' has smaller leaves and denser branching. In early spring, the new leaves emerge soft red, fading to pink and then mid-green in summer. In autumn, the foliage turns red. Small leaves and a twiggy habit make this a much sought-after bonsai.

'DESHŌJŌ': Easily the most popular of all forms of Japanese maple, 'Deshōjō' is an easy-to-keep and eye-catching cultivar. The foliage is a clear, bright red in spring, darkening as it matures and turning green in summer. Before they fall in autumn, the leaves turn pink. The foliage is unaffected by late spring frosts.

'SEIGAI': Another popular cultivar is 'Seigai', but not for the beginner. It has the reputation of being difficult to grow in the temperate climates of Europe and North America, although there are no

Left: The leaves of *Acer palmatum* 'Seigai' have long lobes and emerge a delicate pink in spring. The foliage shown here is the deeper colour of mid-summer.

problems in Japan or or countries that have a Mediterranean climate, where winters are milder. New leaves will be scorched by frost and cold winds in spring, so protect plants in an unheated greenhouse in winter and early spring. The leaves have long, elegant lobes, and in spring are a soft, luminescent pink. As the year progresses they turn reddish-brown and then deep green, with mottled vein patterns.

'SHISHIO': Very similar to 'Deshōjō' is 'Shishio' (syn. 'Chisio'). Its red spring leaves retain their colouring a little longer than 'Deshōjō', before turning green in summer. The leaves change to red again in autumn.

Where to keep them

Treat these cultivars in the same way as *A. palmatum* (see pages 112–13). They enjoy being in full sun in spring and summer, and they can (with the exception of 'Seigai') be left outside in winter as long as the temperature does not fall below

-5°C (23°F). Placing the plants in full sun hardens the leaves and twigs; allowing the foliage to emerge in the open air produces a better, clearer red in spring. If plants are kept in a greenhouse in spring, the leaves tend to be a duller shade of red.

How to look after them

Treat these cultivars in same way as *A. palmatum*, except for 'Seigai', which needs protection from frost and cold winds when new foliage emerges during spring.

Acer palmatum 'Deshōjō'

Acer palmatum cultivars

Japanese maple varieties 2

- *hardy*
- *deciduous*
- *easy to train*
- *different colours/ shapes*
- *novelty plants*

Many other hardy cultivars of Japanese maple are grown as bonsai, and most of these are available from nurseries in Europe, Australia, New Zealand, South Africa, North and South America – large quantities being exported from Japan and China. Some are described below. Most are fairly easy to shape, and are treated in the same way as *Acer palmatum* (see pages 112– 13).

'AKA SHIGITATSU-SAWA' (SYN. 'BENI-SHIGITATSU-SAWA'): The leaves of this cultivar are particularly attractive because of their distinctive vein patterning. It is the red form of the variegated 'Shigitatsu-sawa'.

'ARAKAWA': Its rough, corky bark gives an ancient, rugged appearance. In spring the new leaves are bronze, becoming a spectacular bright scarlet in autumn. The trunk tends to rot on older specimens.

'ASAHI-ZURU': This cultivar is grown mainly for its pink, cream and pale green spring foliage. In summer, the pink hues fade, and the leaves tend to burn in strong sunshine. The branches are stiff and difficult to train. 'Asahi-zuru' is prone to twig die-back; if this occurs, prune back hard to healthy tissue.

'HIGA-SAYAMA': The spring foliage is very attractive (pale green leaves, edged with cream and pink) and the tips of the leaves curl upwards. Leaves lose some of the variegation in summer and turn red in autumn.

'KASHIMA-YATSUBUSA': A popular dwarf Japanese maple with small leaves, twiggy branch structure and upright habit. It

Above: The dwarf cultivar *Acer palmatum* 'Kiyohime' produces fine, small leaves.

will benefit from leaf pruning and regular branch thinning, to prevent die-back.

'KIYOHIME': This dwarf cultivar is extensively used and almost invariably grown in the broom style. It has small leaves and a dense, twiggy branch structure. Thin the branches regularly. Leaf prune strong, healthy trees in early summer. This is one of the earliest maples to come into leaf, so repotting should be done early (about a couple of weeks before the other types of Japanese maple).'Kiyohime' fares better in deeper containers than those in which it is usually sold.

'KOTO-NO-ITO': The name of this cultivar means 'harp string', and its leaves are like fine threads or the strings of a Japanese harp. The pale green leaves of early spring turn bright red in autumn.

Acer palmatum 'Kashima-yatsubusa'

'KURUI-JISHI': This cultivar is grown primarily for the novelty value of its curled, misshapen leaves.

'MIKAWA-YATSUBUSA': The mid-green leaves of this dwarf form grow in tight, congested bunches and turn red in autumn. It is difficult to train.

A. PALMATUM VAR. DISSECTUM

'SEIRYŪ': The delicate foliage is bronze in spring, pale green in summer and red in autumn.

'SHIGI-TATSU-SAWA': This cultivar bears variegated foliage, with clearly visible veins. The leaves turn red in autumn.

'SHISHIGASHIRA': This maple has tight foliage, which is particularly attractive, and the small leaves make it very suitable for bonsai. Shaping is normally done by pruning alone.

'UKON': The pale lime-green foliage turns to pure gold in autumn.

Aesculus hippocastanum

Horse chestnut, Buckeye

- *hardy*
- *deciduous*
- *easy to train*
- *white or red flowers*
- *novelty tree*

Horse chestnut is not often used for bonsai, but when trained well it forms an eye-catching plant that is particularly suitable for the formal upright, informal upright and natural tree styles. It has mid-green leaves consisting of five to seven leaflets. White flowers are borne in upright clusters in late spring to early summer. Although not sold commercially as a bonsai, the species is popular with enthusiasts of novelty trees. There are several cultivars, including some with double flowers and some with red flowers.

Where to keep them

Horse chestnut (zones 5–6) is native to south-eastern Europe. It is generally hardy, but should be moved to a frost-free greenhouse or shed if long periods of very low temperatures are forecast. During summer, position horse chestnut out of direct sun, which will otherwise scorch the foliage.

How to look after them

REPOTTING: Horse chestnut does not need to be repotted too frequently, because this encourages the leaves to get large. Once every 3–5 years is sufficient. Repotting is best done in early spring. Do not overpot – that is, do not use too large a pot – because this also encourages large leaves. Horse

Above: This is the full-size leaf of horse chestnut when trained as a bonsai. The spotting on the leaf is typical of this species.

chestnut prefers free-draining compost that is rich in loam.

PRUNING AND PINCHING: Prune the tips of the shoots (the sticky buds) before the leaves emerge, to encourage a good overall branch structure. To keep the silhouette neat, pinch out the growing tips of new shoots when two or three leaves have formed, continuing to do this throughout the growing season. Leaf size can be reduced through leaf pruning (total or partial defoliation; see page 30) in early summer. This will induce a new crop of smaller leaves.

WIRING: Horse chestnut is shaped mainly by pruning. If you wish to wire, do so in mid-summer, when the twigs have just hardened. Leave the wires on for a maximum of one growing season.

WATERING: Horse chestnut loses a lot of water, particularly in the growing season, through transpiration. You therefore need to water twice a day in hot, sunny weather. Keep the soil just moist during winter.

FEEDING: Take care to apply weak solutions of a general liquid fertilizer, in spring, because too strong a fertilizer will burn the leaves.

BE AWARE: Horse chestnut tends to shed its leaves early – sometimes in late summer – although leaf pruning carried out in early summer can help to prolong the season. Nevertheless, by late summer a horse chestnut bonsai will often begin to look tired. Scale insects can be a problem; apply a systemic insecticide, if necessary. Horse chestnut is also susceptible to canker, coral spot and leaf blotch. Pick off and destroy infected leaves or wood, and apply a fungicide. A winter wash of lime sulphur may help prevent such diseases.

Aesculus hippocastanum

Alnus
Alder

- *hardy*
- *decidous*
- *easy to train*
- *trouble free*
- *yellow-brown catkins*

Alnus cordata (Italian alder) and *A. glutinosa* (common alder, black alder) are grown as bonsai. Italian alder has glossy, dark green, heart-shaped leaves, while common alder bears dark green, ovate leaves. Both species produce yellowish-brown catkins in late winter or early spring. They make attractive bonsai, although the leaves can appear out of proportion to the tree. Alders are easy to train but are rarely seen in commercial bonsai nurseries, being preferred by amateur enthusiasts.

Where to keep them

Italian alder (zone 5) is native to southern Italy, and common alder (zone 5) is found throughout Europe and into north Africa and western Asia. Both are

hardy species, although they should be moved to a frost-free greenhouse or shed if prolonged freezing weather is forecast. In summer, place in full sun.

How to look after them

REPOTTING: Both alders are vigorous plants and should be repotted annually in early spring. They are not fussy about the compost used. When repotting, you can remove up to half the rootball.

PRUNING AND PINCHING: During spring, prune back to old wood to maintain

Left: The dark green, ovate leaves of fast-growing common alder are distinct from the heart-shaped foliage of Italian alder.

the plant's structure. Alders grow very rapidly, so Italian alder and common alder need regular pruning in summer if they are to stay in good shape. You should pinch out the tips of new shoots weekly during the growing season, to keep the tree compact and promote short internodes.

WIRING: Wire the previous year's growth, which will have had time to harden, because the new growth is usually too tender. Remove the wires as soon as the branches have set in position, which may take just a couple of months. Alder marks easily from wiring, but this is not necessarily detrimental, because a rough, scarred surface lends character to the bonsai.

WATERING: Water Italian alder and common alder freely throughout the growing season. Common alder, which is often found near water in the wild, tolerates wet compost for short periods of time. In winter, keep the compost for both species just moist, to avoid rot.

FEEDING: Apply a general fertilizer once a month from early spring to late summer.

BE AWARE: Alders are occasionally infested with aphids and scale insect;

when necessary, apply a systemic insecticide. Although the plants like moisture-retentive soil, if alders stand in waterlogged soil for too long they suffer from root rot, a fatal disease. Branches are sometimes prone to die-back; when this occurs, prune back to healthy tissue.

Alnus glutinosa

Betula

Birch

- hardy
- deciduous
- more challenging
- delicate branches
- white bark

The Chinese and Japanese have never used birches for their bonsai, but two species, *Betula pendula* (silver birch) and *B. utilis* (Himalayan birch), are increasingly trained by enthusiasts in temperate regions the world over, for forest plantings and individual specimen bonsai. It takes a long while before the bark turns white, but it will eventually do so. Birches are not usually sold as commercial bonsai, but they are available from amateur enthusiasts and through societies.

Where to keep them

Silver birch (zones 2–3) is found growing throughout Europe and Russia, while Himalayan birch (zones 2–3) is native to China and the Himalayas, so these hardy trees need no winter protection. In summer, they can be placed in full sun or partial shade. Unfortunately, birches are not as long-lived as bonsai, because the trunks rot easily; try replanting them in open ground from time to time to rejuvenate tired specimens.

How to look after them

REPOTTING: Repot birches once every 3–4 years. This is best done in early spring. Use a well-drained, but moisture-retentive compost consisting of equal parts loam, peat (or garden compost) and sharp sand.

PRUNING AND PINCHING: Cut birch bonsai back to old wood each spring,

Above: The bark on silver birch turns its distinctive shade of white only when the trees are at least ten years old.

to encourage new shoots. Prune silver birch and Himalayan birch regularly throughout spring and summer to encourage fine branching. Pinch out the growing tips of new shoots when two or three leaves have formed, continuing to do this throughout the growing season.

WIRING: If necessary, the major branches can be wired, to emphasize the shape, but there is rarely any need to do this. If you have to wire branches, wire only those that have hardened slightly. Wiring newly formed shoots can cause the shoot to die back, and wiring during winter (when the wires will chill the plant) may have the same effect. Do not leave wires on for more than a year, because they may mark the tree.

WATERING: Birches need daily watering from spring to autumn. On hot, sunny days they require watering twice daily. In winter, the compost should be kept only just moist.

FEEDING: Apply a weak general fertilizer once a month in the growing season.

BE AWARE: Apply a systemic fungicide if aphids are a problem. Branch die-back is common with silver birch and Himalayan birch; cut back infected wood hard to

healthy tissue, then prune to develop a new framework of branches. Birches are also susceptible to the serious disease honey fungus, which must be treated with a fungicide as soon as symptoms are noticed.

Betula pendula

Buxus

Boxwood, Box

- *fairly hardy*
- *evergreen shrub*
- *easy to grow and train*
- *need to be fed regularly*
- *nice bark*

Buxus, a large genus of more than 70 species of evergreen shrubs, is used extensively as an ornamental plant in garden schemes, particularly for hedging and topiary. With its small, glossy, evergreen leaves it makes excellent bonsai. The hard, long-lasting wood can be carved and used for driftwood effects.

Above: Box has leathery leaves, which are green in summer but can turn slightly yellow with the onset of winter.

Where to keep them

Boxwood (zones 4–9) can be grown in both sun and partial shade, but it will have a deeper green if given some shade. Varieties such as *B. harlandii*, which come from southern China as bonsai, can be troublesome, because they are not hardy in temperate climates. This species grows best in tropical and subtropical ones. If in doubt, provide winter protection.

How to look after them

REPOTTING: Boxwood trees have vigorous root systems, so need repotting every other year, but check the rootball first in case it is not pot bound. They prefer a well-drained, neutral to slightly alkaline compost with lots of organic matter in it. The optimum time to repot is from early to mid-spring.

PRUNING AND PINCHING: Prune boxwood with scissors rather than by pinching out the young shoots. As all boxwood are hedging plants, they stand up well to regular pruning.

WIRING: Much of the shaping can be achieved without the use of wire – just pruning is sufficient. Also, as the wood is quite hard, wiring can be difficult.

WATERING: Boxwood does not require lots of water, but the soil should be kept moist and damp.

FEEDING: Use a high-nitrogen fertilizer in spring and early summer, and a general one in mid-summer.

BE AWARE: Some varieties of boxwood suffer from a disease called box blight, in which branches die suddenly, for no apparent reason. If this occurs, just cut the dead branches out and burn the diseased parts. Some boxwood varieties turn reddish-brown in winter when exposed to frost. This may not kill the plant, and the colour will turn green again with feeding in spring.

Buxus sempervirens

Carpinus betulus

Common hornbeam

- *hardy*
- *decidous*
- *fast growing*
- *easy to train*
- *attractive, pyramidal shape*
- *fluted bark*

Common hornbeam is often used for hedging in gardens, but it also makes an attractive feature plant, having an upright, pyramidal habit. The mid-green leaves are toothed and turn yellow in autumn, before they fall. Yellow and green catkins are borne in spring. This tree needs no special care, and can be trained into a bonsai in many styles.

Where to keep them

Common hornbeam (zones 4–5), which is native to Europe, Turkey and Ukraine, is hardy and needs no winter protection. In summer, mature plants do best in full sun, although young plants benefit from a little shade in mid-summer.

How to look after them

REPOTTING: Repot every 3–4 years in early spring, but only when the rootball is pot bound. Repotting too frequently will result in large, coarse leaves and long internodes. Common hornbeam is not fussy about compost, although a free-draining, multi-purpose mix of equal parts loam, peat (or garden compost) and sharp sand is best.

PRUNING AND PINCHING: Heavy branches can be pruned at any time of year, although this is best done in summer when any cuts will heal quickly. In spring and summer, encourage fine branching by regularly pruning back

Left: The leaves of common hornbeam are attractive but vulnerable to scorching in summer; protect them by keeping the plant well watered.

shoots. Pinch out the growing tips of new shoots as soon as two or three leaves have formed, and continue to do this, as necessary, throughout the growing season.

WIRING: Rarely used to shape common hornbeam, wiring can, if necessary, be done in spring and summer. The wires can be left on for about a year on young branches and for two to three years on older, thicker branches.

WATERING: Water freely twice a day in mid-summer, and once a day in spring and autumn. Keep the compost just moist in winter.

FEEDING: Feed common hornbeam once every other month with a weak solution of a general fertilizer. Overfeeding will cause branches to thicken unduly, and the leaves to become large and coarse.

BE AWARE: Treat aphids with a systemic insecticide. Remove caterpillars by hand. Common hornbeam is also susceptible to leaf spot, a fungal disease. Pick off and destroy infected leaves and apply a fungicide. Also avoid spraying or misting plants that are standing in direct sun.

*Carpinus
betulus*

Carpinus laxiflora

Japanese hornbeam

- *hardy*
- *deciduous*
- *delicate shape*
- *beautiful bark*
- *vivid autumn colour*

Japanese hornbeam is a much more delicate tree than its European cousin *Carpinus betulus* (see pages 126–7). It has fine, mid-green, pointed leaves, which turn beautiful shades of orange and pink in autumn. The bark is particularly lovely – pale grey with dark, vertical striations – which means that the trees are particularly attractive in winter, when they are without their leaves. The graceful habit of Japanese hornbeam makes it ideal for forest and group plantings, and they are also excellent individual specimens in the twin and multi-trunk styles.

This species does not grow as vigorously as common hornbeam. If a thick trunk is required, plant your specimen in open ground for a couple of years, to produce the desired effect.

Where to keep them

Japanese hornbeam (zones 4–5), which is native to Japan and Korea, is hardy in temperate areas but benefits from being moved to a frost-free greenhouse or shed in prolonged spells of cold weather. Place in full sun in early summer, and in partial shade during the hot mid-summer.

How to look after them

REPOTTING: Repot Japanese hornbeam every 3–4 years in early spring, but

Left: The leaves of Japanese hornbeam are much finer than those of common hornbeam. They are also more colourful in autumn.

only when the rootball is pot bound. Use a free-draining, multi-purpose mix of equal parts loam, peat (or garden compost) and sharp sand.

PRUNING AND PINCHING: Heavy branches can be pruned at any time of year, although they are best severed in summer, when any cuts will heal quickly. In spring and summer, encourage a fine branch structure by regularly pruning back shoots. Pinch out the growing tips of new shoots as soon as two or three leaves have formed. Continue throughout the growing season as necessary.

WIRING: Although the bonsai shape is usually achieved by pruning, if wiring is necessary apply wire only to twigs and branches that have become firm. Those produced in the current season are too delicate for wiring. The wires can be left on for about a year on young branches and 2–3 years on older, thicker ones.

WATERING: Water generously throughout the growing season, and never let the compost dry out. Reduce watering with the onset of autumn. Keep the compost just moist in winter.

FEEDING: Between early spring and late summer, feed sparingly once a month with a general fertilizer.

BE AWARE: Fine branches tend to die back for no apparent reason. When this happens, cut back to healthy tissue. Treat aphids with a systemic insecticide.

Carpinus laxiflora

Carpinus turczaninowii

Korean hornbeam

- *hardy*
- *deciduous*
- *easy to grow and train*
- *elegant shape*
- *green catkins*

This is perhaps the most highly sought after of all the hornbeams. It is an elegant tree with slightly rounded, toothed, glossy dark green leaves, which turn salmon-pink in autumn. Green and yellowish-green catkins are borne in spring. Specimens with thick trunks are particularly impressive. Regular pruning will soon produce an attractive structure of twigs and branches. Good specimens tend to be expensive but are available from most bonsai nurseries. Korean hornbeam is much appreciated by enthusiasts, as it can be carved with power tools to create striking hollow-trunk effects (see page 33).

Where to keep them

Korean hornbeam (zones 3–5) is native to China, Japan and Korea, and it is hardy in all temperate areas, although it appreciates being moved to a frost-free greenhouse or shed during prolonged periods of extremely cold weather. This species does best if it is kept out in the open in full sun for the duration of the growing season.

How to look after them

REPOTTING: Repot Korean hornbeam once every 2–3 years in early spring, but only when the rootball is pot bound.

Left: The leaves of Korean hornbeam are smaller and more rounded than those of Japanese and common hornbeam.

You should use a free-draining, multi-purpose mix of equal parts loam, peat (or garden compost) and sharp sand. When repotting, do not remove more than one-third of the rootball.

PRUNING AND PINCHING: Heavy branches can be pruned at any time of year, although this is best done in summer, when any cuts will heal quickly. In spring and summer, encourage a fine branch structure by regularly pruning back shoots. Pinch out the growing tips of new shoots as soon as two or three leaves have formed. Continue to do this, as necessary, throughout the growing season.

WIRING: Branches can be wired in early spring, if necessary. The wires can be left on for about a year on young branches and 2–3 years on the older, thicker ones.

WATERING: Keep the tree well watered during the growing season, watering once a day in spring and autumn and twice a day in mid-summer, if necessary. In winter, keep the compost just moist.

FEEDING: Apply a general fertilizer in spring and early summer, but in late summer change to a low-nitrogen one.

BE AWARE: This is a robust species, which is not susceptible to disease and is rarely attacked by aphids or scale insects. If the plant is infested, apply a systemic insecticide.

Carpinus turczaninowii

Conocarpus erectus

Buttonwood

- *popular evergreen in the USA*
- *easy to keep and train*
- *excellent for carving driftwood effects*

Buttonwood is a typical American species for bonsai, but is seldom used outside that country. It is an evergreen shrub bearing shiny leaves and small, insignificant flowers, which develop into little, brown fruits. Its shrubby nature and contorted branches lend themselves to bonsai, especially driftwood effects. This very lovely tree is commonly available in US nurseries and garden centres.

Where to keep them

This is really a tropical or subtropical species (zones 10–11). Buttonwood does not do at all well in cold climates. Keep plants in as much sun as possible. Protect from frost in winter.

How to look after them

REPOTTING: Repot this vigorous grower in late spring or early summer. It likes warm balmy nights after repotting, If you repot too early in the growing season, the roots may have difficulty recovering. Use a very free-draining compost, because buttonwood does not like to be waterlogged.

Left: Buttonwood bears lovely evergreen leaves and pale white flowers.

PRUNING AND PINCHING: Prune shoots in mid-summer. Buttonwood loves frequent pruning, and this will produce a good framework. It can also be leaf pruned (see page 30), but be careful as this can sometimes cause branch die-back. If in doubt, do not leaf prune.

WIRING: Wire buttonwood bonsais in mid-summer. Wrap the wire in paper, because the summer sun can damage branches from the heat transmitted through the wires.

WATERING: Apply lots of water in the growing season. Water slightly less at other times of the year.

FEEDING: Feed once a month with a general fertilizer in the growing season.

BE AWARE: Look out for aphids, mites and fluffy scale or mealy bug. If you use insecticide, apply at half strength. Treat all driftwood with lime sulphur.

Conocarpus erectus

Fagus

Beech

- *hardy*
- *deciduous*
- *easy to train*
- *elegant shapes*
- *interesting bark*

Two species of beech are popular for bonsai and suitable for most styles: *Fagus sylvatica* (common beech) and *F. crenata* (Japanese white beech). Common beech is widely used by enthusiasts in cool-temperate regions, while Japanese white beech is preferred in Japan. Common beech tends to have large leaves, pale green at first, deepening to dark green and turning yellow or orange-brown before they fall in spring, just before the new leaves appear. This species has greyish-brown bark. Japanese white beech is a more elegant tree, with smaller, mid-green leaves, which turn yellow in autumn, and stunning, white bark.

Where to keep them

Beeches are native to temperate areas in the northern hemisphere. Japanese white bark (zones 6– 7) is native to Japan and should be protected in a frost-free greenhouse or shed in prolonged periods of very cold weather. Common beech (zone 4) is completely hardy, although, as with all bonsai, nothing is lost by moving plants into a frost-free position if you are in any doubt. Both these species of beech can be grown in full sun in summer as long as they never dry out, but at the height

Above: The leaves of common beech (shown here) are rounded, while those of Japanese white beech tend to be more pointed and serrated.

of summer they will benefit from some shade from direct sun.

How to look after them

REPOTTING: Repot every third or fourth year, during early spring. Use compost consisting of equal parts loam and sand, although beeches are tolerant of a wide range of soil types as long as the soil never becomes waterlogged.

PRUNING AND PINCHING: Beeches can be pruned at any time during the growing season. Pinch out the growing tips of new shoots as soon as two leaves have formed. If the twig structure has become very dense, prune in early spring, before the leaves emerge, so that you can see the framework.

WIRING: Beeches are usually shaped by pruning, but if wiring is necessary it can be done between spring and autumn. Because the bark is such an attractive feature of these trees, protect it with raffia before applying the wire. Remove the wires at the end of summer.

WATERING: Regular and plentiful watering throughout summer is essential, because beeches lose a lot

Fagus crenata

of water through transpiration. If the compost dries out, the leaves will wither and turn brown. If this happens, cut off the dried leaves, to encourage new shoots to form. Keep the compost just moist in winter.

FEEDING: Apply a high-nitrogen fertilizer in spring, changing to a low-nitrogen one in late summer.

BE AWARE: Beeches suffer from aphids and scale insects, which can be treated with a systemic insecticide. The branches are also susceptible to die-back if they do not receive adequate light. If this happens, cut back to healthy tissue.

Fraxinus

Ash

- *hardy*
- *deciduous*
- *fast growing*
- *easy to keep*
- *scented, white flowers*

This is a large genus, but the species grown as bonsai are *Fraxinus americana* (white ash), *F. excelsior* (common ash) and *F. ornus* (manna ash). These are suitable for most styles of bonsai, and make especially nice literati and forest groups. All have pinnate, mid- to dark green leaves, which change colour in autumn before falling. Manna ash bears clusters of fragrant, white flowers in late spring to early summer. Although ashes are not normally used as ornamental trees in the garden, they nevertheless make attractive bonsai and are used by amateur enthusiasts.

Unfortunately, ash specimens are rarely available from commercial bonsai outlets. However, these are extremely vigorous trees, and thick trunk specimens can be produced easily by growing them in the open ground or in large growing boxes. Where ash grows wild in suburban gardens, the seedlings are so prolific that they are considered by many gardeners as weeds – but they make ideal bonsai material.

Where to keep them

White ash, common ash and manna ash (all zones 3– 4) are all native to temperate areas in the northern hemisphere and so are perfectly hardy, needing no special

Left: The fresh-looking, bright green leaves are a particularly attractive feature of common ash bonsai.

protection in winter. In summer, these plants can be kept in full sun.

How to look after them

REPOTTING: Ashes are vigorous trees and will need repotting every year or at least every other year. The best time to do this is during early spring. They prefer neutral to alkaline, moisture-retentive but well-drained compost.

PRUNING AND PINCHING: Prune ash back in spring, before the leaves emerge, so that you can assess the branch structure. These fast-growing trees are easy to train through pruning: repeated cutting of the apex will soon develop a good tapering trunk, and frequent trimming of the secondary shoots will produce a good branch framework. Prune constantly to keep trees compact. Pinch out the growing tip of new shoots as soon as two or three leaves have formed.

WIRING: If necessary, wiring can be done at any time of the year. The wires should not be left on for longer than a growing season.

WATERING: Water regularly throughout the growing season, making sure that the soil never dries out, which will lead to leaf drop or die-back. In winter, keep the compost just moist.

FEEDING: Apply a general fertilizer once or twice a year in the growing season. Ashes are not greedy plants.

BE AWARE: Look out for telltale symptoms of ash die-back, such as twigs dying for no obvious reason. Burn infected trees.

Fraxinus excelsior

Ginkgo biloba
Maidenhair tree, Ichō

- *hardy*
- *deciduous*
- *more challenging*
- *vivid colour*
- *flowers and fruit*

Ginkgo biloba is one of the oldest species of tree to have survived from ancient times, although it is now extinct in the wild. The species is highly prized as bonsai in China and Japan, because of its beautiful leaves, which turn yellow in autumn, and because these trees can live to a great age. Male and female flowers are borne on separate trees: male flowers resemble catkins, while the rounded female blooms are followed by plum-like fruits. Most ginkgos are trained in the flame shape, which is how they grow naturally. They are available as bonsai from specialist nurseries or as nursery material for training.

Where to keep them

Ginkgo (zone 4) is native to southern China and is perfectly hardy, requiring no special protection in winter, although late spring frosts sometimes damage new shoots. Keep it in an unheated greenhouse or shed if frost is forecast during this time. It tolerates full sun, although young shoots may be scorched by direct sun in mid-summer and will benefit from partial shade.

Right: The leaves of ginkgo change from green to rich golden yellow in autumn. No other tree has such unusual and lovely foliage.

How to look after them

REPOTTING: Repot every 3–4 years, in early spring. When doing so, use compost consisting of two parts loam, one part peat (or garden compost) and one part sharp sand.

PRUNING AND PINCHING: Prune old wood in early spring, before the new leaves emerge. Be aware that constant pruning can encourage suckers to proliferate. Pinch out the growing tips of new shoots on the trunk and main branches when two or three leaves have formed on each shoot, continuing to do this throughout the growing season.

WIRING: Ginkgo does not usually need wiring because it is grown in the flame shape, which is the natural habit of growth of this species.

WATERING: Water regularly from spring to late autumn, and in winter keep the compost just moist. The foliage will benefit from regular misting in summer.

FEEDING: From spring to late summer apply a general fertilizer, changing to a low-nitrogen one for the last autumn feeds.

BE AWARE: Although ginkgo is largely trouble free, aphids are often attracted to the new leaves. If there are too many to remove by hand, apply a systemic insecticide, at the rate recommended by the manufacturer.

Ginkgo biloba

Hedera

Ivy

- *evergreen*
- *easy from cuttings*
- *more difficult to train into good bonsai*
- *unusual as bonsai – always a talking point*

Ivy is a widely distributed genus of about 15 species of evergreen climber. Although a native of Europe and western Asia, it now grows in any country that has a temperate or subtropical climate. These extremely vigorous climbers develop thick trunks once they establish themselves on walls and trees. Ivy makes interesting bonsai when the trunks are gnarled and old, and quite a few of the variegated varieties work well. These are very much hobbyist's plants and are not often sold as bonsai by commercial nurseries.

Where to keep them

Ivies (zones 3–9) are hardy in temperate regions, but benefit from some protection during winter. Grow in partial shade.

How to look after them

REPOTTING: Ivies do not need repotting often, and pot-bound plants have smaller leaves. They are not fussy about compost, because they grow in any soil.

PRUNING AND PINCHING: Pinch out the new shoots regularly during the growing season.

WIRING: The floppy branches or shoots need the support of wires to create

Above: All ivies develop nice thick trunks when trained as bonsai. Even a small bonsai such as this one has a characterful trunk.

interesting shapes. Ivy can be wired
at any time of the year.

WATERING: Water regularly in summer.
Do not let the compost dry out.

FEEDING: Feed a half-strength general
fertilizer in summer. Avoid overfeeding,
as it will result in large leaves.

BE AWARE: Scale and other insect
pests can be a problem. Physically
remove these pests or
apply an appropriate
insecticide.

Hedera helix

Ilex aquifolium

Common holly

- *moderately hardy evergreen*
- *not common as bonsai*
- *challenging subject*
- *coloured berries*

Common holly is native to Europe, west Asia and north Africa. It is a beautiful evergreen tree with glossy, dark green leaves and red berries. Numerous cultivars have been bred in recent years – some with smooth-edged or variegated leaves, while others bear yellow or orange berries. Berries are harmful if ingested by humans, but are an important source of food for birds in winter. Common holly is not often sold as bonsai commercially, but it does make interesting bonsai, nonetheless.

Above: For many people, the attractive red fruit of common holly is associated with Christmas.

Where to keep them

Although common holly (zones 6–9) is a hardy plant, you should provide some protection from hard frosts in winter, because the roots are tender when grown as bonsai. Keep in full sun or semi-shade, and protect from direct sunlight during very hot summer days.

How to look after them

REPOTTING: Repot every 3–4 years when roots become pot bound. Common holly is not fussy about the soil in which it grows.

PRUNING AND PINCHING: Prune new shoots during the growing season.

If you want flowers and berries the following year, do not remove any of the current season's growth.

WIRING: This is best done in winter or early spring. The spiny leaf varieties are difficult to wire, so exercise care.

WATERING: Water moderately but do not let the tree dry out completely.

FEEDING: Feed with a high-nitrogen fertilizer in spring and a low-nitrogen one in late summer.

BE AWARE: Scale and aphids can be a problem, so be vigilant and pick them off by hand or spray with an insecticide.

Ilex aquifolium

143

Ligustrum vulgare

Common privet

- *hardy*
- *deciduous/ semi-evergreen*
- *easy to train*
- *impressive trunk*

Common privet is widely used for hedging in gardens, but single plants make attractive bonsai, and in recent years bonsai enthusiasts have demonstrated that ordinary plants such as this have the potential to become outstanding bonsai specimens. Not only is this species easy to grow, but the plant itself also has many fine qualities. The trunk is impressive and lends itself to driftwood effects (see page 33); the leaves are small and neat; and branches can be wired easily. This species is very suitable for the informal upright style.

Common pivet is not grown commercially for outdoor bonsai, although other species may be grown indoors (see pages 282– 3). Nurseries may sell the raw material for making this plant into bonsai.

Where to keep them

Common privet (zones 4– 6), which is native to a wide area of Europe, north Africa and south-western Asia, is completely hardy in temperate climates and, therefore, requires no special protection in the winter months. During summer, it can be kept in full sun.

Above: Like most hedging plants, common privet is a prolific grower. It produces small-scale leaves, which are ideal for bonsai.

How to look after them

REPOTTING: Repot common privet each year if the roots become pot bound, but otherwise every other year will be enough. The best time to do this is early spring. Use any well-drained but moisture-retentive compost.

PRUNING AND PINCHING: Common privet is extremely fast growing and vigorous. Hard pruning can be done at any time of year, but is best in summer, when cuts heal quickly. Cut back to the main trunk, if necessary. You will need to trim the shoots regularly to maintain the overall shape of the plant, and constant pinching out of the tips of new shoots will be required during the growing season. If you want to carve thick trunks to resemble the hollow trunks found in nature, do so in spring or summer.

WIRING: Branches can be wired at any time of the year. Wire shoots that have been formed in the current season and do not leave the wires on the plant for longer than one season.

WATERING: Water regularly from spring to late autumn, but allow the surface of the soil to dry between each watering. Keep the compost just moist in winter.

FEEDING: This species is not a greedy feeder, and two applications of a general fertilizer – one in spring and one in late summer – should be sufficient.

BE AWARE: Aphids and scale insects can be a problem. Apply a systemic insecticide if you cannot pick off all the pests by hand.

Ligustrum vulgare

Liquidambar styraciflua

Sweet gum, Liquid amber

- *hardy, deciduous tree*
- *attractive autumn foliage*
- *easy to train and keep as bonsai*

Sweet gum, also known as liquid amber, exudes a sweet resin. It grows in temperate and subtropical climates and is commonly found in the south-eastern United States. The leaves resemble those of *Acer palmatum* (see pages 112–17), but unlike this species sweet gum develops corky bark and twigs. Like *Acer palmatum*, sweet gum has stunning autumn colours, which usually occur after the first frosts.

Where to keep them

Although typically a temperate climate tree (zones 5–9), sweet gum grows well in subtropical climates too. Being a hardy tree, it does not need winter protection if grown in milder temperate regions. If winters are extreme, protect sweet gum from hard frosts. It needs full sun.

How to look after them

REPOTTING: Repot every couple of years when roots become pot bound. Use slightly acid compost.

PRUNING AND PINCHING: Pinch out new growth in mid-summer, to keep the bonsai compact. Do not allow long shoots to develop, because they spoil the shape of the tree. Regular pruning encourages the development of new twigs and branches.

WIRING: The trunk and branches can be wired but be careful not to damage

Above: The autumn foliage of sweet gum is deep crimson – like that of Japanese maple.

the corky bark and wings that grow on the branches, as they are an attractive feature of the tree.

WATERING: Water once a day in the spring and autumn, and twice daily in the summer. Watering in strong sunshine will not burn sweet gum leaves. Reduce watering slightly in late summer or early autumn, because excessive watering can result in soft lush growth, which will not colour well.

FEEDING: Start feeding from mid- to late spring, using a high-nitrogen fertilizer; in mid-summer switch to a low-nitrogen fertilizer, to help the leaves develop good autumn colour.

BE AWARE: Sweet gum is susceptible to scale insects, and its leaves can get fungal infection. Spray with an appropriate insecticide or fungicide when symptoms occur.

Liquidambar styraciflua

Lonicera nitida

Hedging honeysuckle

- *hardy*
- *semi-evergreen*
- *easy to train*
- *neat outline*
- *white flowers*

This species is in the same genus as the well-known flowering climbers, but it is a small, neat shrub, widely used for hedging in gardens but with many characteristics that make it a suitable bonsai. The small, glossy leaves are dark green above and lighter beneath. Small, white flowers appear in spring and are followed by purple-blue berries. Old plants can develop thick trunks, which make them ideal for small and medium-sized specimen bonsai. They are also suitable for carving driftwood effects (see page 33) and can be trained into most bonsai styles.

Above: Even the full-size leaves of hedging honeysuckle are small and dainty. The top surfaces of the leaves are dark green, while the undersides are paler.

Although hedging honeysuckle is not used for commercial bonsai, it is popular with amateur enthusiasts and can be trained without difficulty. As it is fast growing, it can be easily propagated from cuttings, and young plants are ideal for the miniature bonsai known as *mame*. Older specimens with thick trunks are usually sourced from hedges and gardens, where they have been growing for a long time.

Where to keep them

Hedging honeysuckle (zones 5–7) is native to south-western China. Although it is generally hardy, it should be moved to a frost-free greenhouse or shed if prolonged periods of freezing weather are forecast. During the growing season, keep in full sun.

How to look after them

REPOTTING: Repot every other year during early spring. Use a free-draining but moisture-retentive compost, consisting of equal parts loam, peat (or garden compost) and sharp sand.

PRUNING AND PINCHING: Regular pruning is essential to maintain the bonsai's shape. The tips of new shoots will need to be constantly pinched out during the growing season. Hard pruning is best done in the summer months, when cuts heal quickly. Cut back to the main trunk, if necessary.

WIRING: If you wish to develop a new branch, simply allow one new bud to grow unchecked until the branch is sufficiently thick. This can be achieved in one growing season and, when thick enough, the branch can be wired. However, there is no real need to wire this species, as all the training can be achieved through pruning.

WATERING: Water hedging honeysuckle regularly in the growing season and never let the soil dry out.

The leaves will drop if the rootball gets too dry. In winter, keep the compost just moist.

FEEDING: Apply a general fertilizer in spring and summer.

BE AWARE: Aphids are the only potential problem likely to trouble these reliable plants. Apply a systemic insecticide if you cannot pick off all of the pests by hand.

Lonicera nitida

Nothofagus antarctica

Antarctic beech

- *hardy*
- *deciduous*
- *easy to train*
- *small leaves*
- *vivid autumn colour*

This small tree or shrub makes a most attractive bonsai subject and is suitable for most styles of bonsai. The small, rounded leaves, which are glossy and dark green, turn a beautiful shade of orange before they fall in autumn. Plants are easy to grow and train. Antarctic beech is popular with amateur enthusiasts, but is not often seen in commercial bonsai nurseries.

Above: Perhaps surprisingly, the attractive leaves of Antarctic beech are reminiscent of those of birch, rather than of beech.

Where to keep them

Antarctic beech (zones 6–7) is native to southern Chile and Argentina, as its common name suggests. It is generally hardy, although plants should be moved to a frost-free greenhouse or shed if long periods of very cold weather are forecast. Shelter young plants from cold, drying winds. In summer, keep Antarctic beech in full sun.

How to look after them

REPOTTING: Repot Antarctic beech every 2–3 years, during early spring. It requires moisture-retentive but free-draining soil, which must be lime-free (ericaceous) or the leaves will become chlorotic, turn yellow and die.

PRUNING AND PINCHING: Plants can be pruned at any time of year. As Antarctic beech has small leaves, you can cut new shoots in whatever way necessary to achieve the outline you want. It is not necessary to trim back to two or three buds, as with species with larger leaves, such as *Fagus* (see pages 134– 5) or *Alnus* (see pages 120– 1). Pinch out the growing tips of new shoots throughout the growing season.

WIRING: Antarctic beech can be wired at any time of the year, although shoots should be wired only when they have hardened sufficiently. Do not leave wires on the branches for longer than a growing season.

WATERING: This species should be watered regularly throughout the growing season. You may need to do this twice a day in summer, to prevent the compost from drying out. In winter, keep the compost just moist.

FEEDING: Apply a general fertilizer in spring, and a low-nitrogen one in late summer.

BE AWARE: These plants are rarely troubled by pests and diseases,

although root rot, which is fatal, occasionally strikes. Never allow roots to become waterlogged.

Nothofagus antarctica

Olea sylvestris

Olive

- *Mediterranean evergreen*
- *needs protection in temperate zones*
- *easy to train and grow*
- *good for carving*

Olive is the iconic genus of the Mediterranean countries, but it also grows in warm-temperate and subtropical regions of the world, such as Africa, Australia and South America. In recent years, many fine examples of olive bonsai have been produced not just in Mediterranean countries but also in countries such as South Africa and Argentina. Olives have attractive, grey-green leaves and tiny, cream-coloured flowers, which develop into the olive fruit. The wood is extremely hard but can be carved with good modern cutting tools. There are many wild species with small leaves, which make excellent bonsai. Many bonsai nurseries in Europe, Africa, Australia, North and South America now stock them, and they propagate easily from cuttings. Fine, old specimens are usually collected from the wild.

Where to keep them

Olives (zones 8–11) can withstand a moderate amount of frost, but, if grown in the temperate region, they need protection from hard frost in winter. They do not like wet soil. Olives love full sun and can tolerate high temperatures.

Left: Olives will flower and fruit prolifically when grown as bonsai. These are the ripe fruit, which develop during autumn.

How to look after them

REPOTTING: Repot every 3–4 years in spring, using free-draining compost.

PRUNING AND PINCHING: Prune in late summer after flowering and when fruits have formed.

WIRING: Olives can be wired at any time although they do not need much wiring as bonsai.

WATERING: As they are Mediterranean plants, olives can withstand some drought. However, they still need to be watered regularly. Let the soil dry out between each watering.

FEEDING: Feed with a general fertilizer in early spring, and with a low-nitrogen fertilizer in mid- and late summer.

BE AWARE: Olives are easy to grow and are not prone to many pest and disease problems. The combination of wet roots and frost is a killer for olive bonsai.

Olea sylvestris

153

Parthenocissus

Virginia creeper

- *hardy, deciduous climber*
- *much-underrated material*
- *enormous potential for bonsai*

There are just a few species in this genus, and they are found mostly in eastern North America and east Asia. They are vigorous, deciduous climbers with three- or five-lobed leaves, which turn deep crimson in autumn. Some varieties of *Parthenocissus quinquefolia* and *P. tricuspidata* (Boston ivy) have variegated foliage. The leaves and berries of this popular garden plant are poisonous. As with most climbing plants, virginia creepers develop characterful trunks when mature and make interesting bonsai. They are popular with hobbyists, because these plants are straightforward to propagate from seed or cuttings and easy to create into bonsai. They are not often sold commercially as bonsai, although some Japanese bonsai nurseries occasionally stock them. It is a good idea to collect old plants from walls and gardens, once you have the owner's permission.

Where to keep them

Virginia creepers (zones 4–9) are not entirely hardy and need some protection from hard frost in winter. Grow in full sun in spring and autumn, but protect from the hot sun during summer.

Left: Virginia creeper foliage turns a lovely crimson in autumn, while the dark purple berries are an additional asset.

Variegated cultivar of
Parthenocissus quinquefolia

How to look after them

REPOTTING: Repot when pot bound,
depending on the vigour of the tree.
Use a deep pot, rather than a shallow
one. Virginia creepers are not fussy
about soil, provided it contains
lots of organic matter.

PRUNING AND PINCHING: Pinch out
the shoot tips regularly
throughout the
growing season.

WIRING: Wiring
is feasible,
but not really
necessary.

WATERING:
Water regularly
in the growing
season. Do not let the
soil dry out completely
in summer.

FEEDING: Feed with a half-strength
general fertilizer in spring, and a
half-strength low-nitrogen one in
late summer.

BE AWARE: Look out for scale
and aphids; treat any infestations
with an appropriate insecticide.

Quercus robur

Common oak, English oak

- hardy
- deciduous
- challenging to train
- attractive bark
- acorns

This species, one of the best-known members of a large genus, develops into a broadly spreading tree, with brownish-grey bark. The familiar, lobed leaves are dark green, and acorns ripen in autumn. When common oak is grown as bonsai, it looks best with a reasonably sized trunk, which takes time to develop. It is particularly suitable for the informal upright style and the broom style. Common oak, which is popular with amateur growers, is not often sold as bonsai in commercial nurseries, although small starter plants can be found and some nurseries have old collected material as partly trained bonsai.

Where to keep them

Common oak (zone 6) is found growing throughout Europe and is hardy, although plants should be moved to a frost-free greenhouse or shed in areas that experience long periods of very cold winter weather. Keep in full sun during summer.

How to look after them

REPOTTING: Common oak prefers to grow in a fairly deep pot. Repot every 2–3 years, during early spring. Use good-quality, moisture-retentive compost consisting of equal parts loam, peat (or garden compost) and sharp sand.

Above: The leaves of common oak look fresh and green in spring, but by mid-summer they can have a tired appearance.

PRUNING AND PINCHING: Any pruning to shape a common oak should be done in early spring, before growth commences. Cut out new shoots, if necessary, in autumn, before the wood has hardened. Because common oak is not a vigorous grower, pinching out is not essential, and the growing bud at the tip of the shoot should be pinched out only when growth has ceased in mid-summer. Leaf pruning (total or partial defoliation; see page 30) can be done in early summer, to induce a second crop of finer leaves.

WIRING: Wire branches in spring or summer, if necessary, although most shaping is achieved by pruning. Take care not to trap leaves under the wires. Retain the wires on the branches for a maximum of a year.

WATERING: Water every day from spring to autumn, increasing the amount given in summer and never allowing the compost to dry out. Keep the compost just moist during winter. Plants enjoy regular misting in summer.

FEEDING: Apply a general fertilizer in spring and late summer. These are not greedy plants.

BE AWARE: Common oak is susceptible to a number of diseases, especially mildew and oak leaf gall, and branches sometimes die back for no apparent reason. Leaf gall is unsightly, but not dangerous, and the best way of dealing with it is simply to remove the affected leaf. If mildew affects the leaves, remove and burn them, then spray the tree with a suitable fungicide. If your tree should suffer from die-back, cut back the branches to healthy tissue.

Quercus robur

Quercus suber

Cork oak

- *half-hardy*
- *evergreen*
- *toothed leaves*
- *corky bark*
- *acorns*

Cork oak is grown chiefly for its thick, corky bark (which is used in the wine trade). It has toothed, dark green leaves and oval acorns. When grown as a bonsai, it looks best as a large specimen, because of the size of its trunk. Cork oak is suitable for most styles, except windswept. Some beautiful examples have been created by bonsai enthusiasts in Italy and Spain, with collected material, but cork oak is not readily available as a young plant or as a bonsai outside Europe.

Where to keep them

Cork oak (zones 7– 10) comes from countries of the western Mediterranean and is not hardy. In Mediterranean countries, trees can be kept in full sun all year, as long as they are protected from the worst of the winter weather. In temperate areas, move them to a heated greenhouse in late autumn and keep them under cover until late spring.

How to look after them

REPOTTING: Cork oak prefers to grow in a fairly deep pot. Repot it every 2– 3 years but only when the roots are pot bound. The best time to do this is during

Above: A mature cork oak bonsai will develop the distinctively gnarled, corky trunk for which larger specimens are prized.

spring, when the buds are about to swell. Use good-quality, moisture-retentive but free-draining compost consisting of equal parts loam, peat (or garden compost) and sharp sand.

PRUNING AND PINCHING: Cork oak can be pruned at any time of year. Pinching out is also required during the growing season, to keep the tree looking trim. Pinch out the growing tips as soon as two or three leaves have appeared. This species also responds well to hard pruning, and a large specimen can be made from nursery material by cutting a tree back to 30–60cm (1–2ft).

WIRING: Wire branches in spring or summer, but apply wire only to shoots from the previous year, which have hardened, to prevent scarring. The wires can be left on for a year.

WATERING: Water cork oak throughout the growing season, increasing the amount of water given in summer. Keep the soil just moist during winter.

FEEDING: Apply a general fertilizer in spring, and again in late summer.

BE AWARE: Cork oak may occasionally be infested by aphids and scale insects, which can be treated with a systemic insecticide if there are too many to remove by hand. Mildew can also be a problem. If the leaves are affected, remove and burn them, then spray with a suitable fungicide.

Quercus suber

Salix babylonica

Weeping willow

- *hardy*
- *deciduous*
- *easy to train*
- *attractive shape*
- *silvery green catkins*

As anyone who has ever grown a weeping willow in the garden will know, this is a vigorous, fast-growing plant with a spreading root system. Weeping willow has slender, mid-green leaves, greyish beneath, and silvery green catkins in spring. It can be used to create attractive bonsai and is one of the few trees that can be trained into the weeping style. Unfortunately, weeping willow is not often seen in commercial bonsai nurseries.

Where to keep them

Weeping willow (zone 5) is native to northern China and is a hardy species that needs no special protection in winter. It can be kept in full sun throughout the growing season.

How to look after them

REPOTTING: This is perhaps the only species that requires repotting twice a year, in early summer and mid-summer. Indeed, it is so vigorous that the roots can sometimes break the pot. Use good-quality, moisture-retentive but free-draining compost consisting of equal parts loam, sharp sand and leaf mould.

PRUNING AND PINCHING: Prune the old branches in early spring, before the sap is circulating, so that the new shoots can be trained to hang down. Pinch back the growing tips of new shoots as

Right: Weeping willow shoots can be encouraged to grow and trail gracefully by pruning back the older shoots hard in early spring.

they emerge, leaving one leaf junction. Continue to do this throughout the growing season.

WIRING: As soon as they have achieved the required length, wire new shoots to train them to weep. You can weight the ends of the stems to create the desired effect. Protect the stems with raffia, to prevent scarring. Retain the wires throughout the growing season.

WATERING: Like all willows, weeping willow must be kept in reliably moist, but not waterlogged, soil. The plant's roots must be able to extract oxygen from the soil if they are to continue to develop, and this is impossible if excess water cannot drain from the soil around the rootball. Keep the soil moist throughout winter.

FEEDING: Apply a weak general fertilizer once a month in the growing season, except in mid-summer or immediately after repotting.

BE AWARE: Aphids are often attracted to the new shoots of a weeping willow, but they can be treated with a systemic insecticide and are rarely a serious problem. Caterpillars, which can defoliate a plant overnight, are more of a pest and should be picked off by hand as soon as they are noticed. If mildew affects the leaves, remove and burn them, then spray the tree with a suitable fungicide.

Salix babylonica

OUTDOOR BROAD-LEAVED BONSAI

Tilia

Lime, Linden

- *unusual deciduous subjects*
- *easy to grow and train*
- *prone to aphids and scale insects*

This is a fairly large genus of temperate, broad-leaved, deciduous trees, which grows in northern Europe, north America and western China. The leaves are a lovely, light green heart shape, and they turn golden in autumn. Flowers are scented. The small-leaved species – in particular *T. cordata* – are very suitable for bonsai and can be trained in most styles except perhaps windswept and literati.

Where to keep them

Limes (zones 3–8) can withstand hard frost, so there is no need to protect them in winter. They may be grown in full sun or partial shade.

How to look after them

REPOTTING: Repot every 2–3 years, in spring, using loamy compost. If limes are repotted too frequently, the leaves will not reduce in size. A careful balance needs to be struck between repotting too frequently and not repotting for five or more years.

Right: The plump red buds of the lime tree are very attractive during winter and early spring when the tree is without its leaves.

162

PRUNING AND PINCHING: Prune in early spring and again in mid-summer, to encourage good framework. On species that have large leaves, leaf pruning (see page 30) in summer will produce a second crop of smaller leaves.

WIRING: Wire at any time, although early spring, before the leaves emerge, is best. Lime bark is soft so do not leave wires on too long, as this will disfigure the branches.

WATERING: Limes like lots of water in summer, less in spring and autumn. Keep just moist in winter.

FEEDING: Feed with a half-strength general fertilizer in midsummer. Heavy feeding will result in large leaves.

BE AWARE: Limes are prone to many types of insect attack. Aphids and fluffy scale are attracted to the leaves and bark in early spring, when they are rich in sap. The leaves are also prone to gall infestation. Treat by leaf pruning, because the second crop of leaves does not usually suffer the fate.

Tilia cordata

Ulmus

Elm

- *versatile*
- *easy to grow*
- *commonly available*
- *easy to train*
- *deciduous*

As with *Juniperus* (see pages 54–71) there are many elm species and varieties that are suitable for bonsai. The elm that is most often seen as bonsai is *Ulmus parvifolia* (see pages 166–7, 310–11). All elms have a wide temperature tolerance range. Local bonsai nurseries are gradually stocking the varieties described here.

U. AMERICANA VAR. FLORIDANA
(FLORIDA ELM): This variety (zones 4–8) of *U. americana* (American elm, white elm) is very popular with hobbyists, especially in Florida and Louisiana. It makes nice bonsai.

U. CRASSIFOLIA (TEXAS CEDAR ELM): Another of the hardy American elms suitable for bonsai is this extremely hardy one (zones 3–10), which grows in Texas and much of southern United States.

U. RUBRA (SLIPPERY ELM): This species (zones 3–10) is native to eastern North America from south-east North Dakota to Maine and southern Quebec, northern Florida and eastern Texas. It makes lovely bonsai, with its slightly larger, velvety leaves. Slippery elm is a good species for American bonsai growers.

Where to keep them

As elms are hardy trees, they may be left outside in winter, but some protection may be necessary if the temperature

U. parvifolia (smooth-bark variety)

falls below -10°C (14°F). All elms enjoy a bright sunny location during summer.

How to look after them

REPOTTING: Repot elms every two or three years in spring, using a general bonsai compost.

PRUNING AND PINCHING: Prune at any time of the year. and pinch out new growth throughout the growing season.

WIRING: Elms can be wired at any time, although they do not need much wiring once the basic shape has been created.

WATERING: Elms need a lot of water during the growing season – on hot days, they may need to be watered twice a day. If they are grown under cover in winter, do not forget to water them because the soil should not be allowed to dry out completely.

FEEDING: Feed with a high-nitrogen fertilizer in spring and early summer. Reduce feeding in mid-summer and use a lower nitrogen feed.

BE AWARE: As far as is known, elm bonsai are not susceptible to Dutch elm disease, the fatal insect-borne disease that affects garden trees.

U. americana var. *floridana*

U. rubra

Ulmus parvifolia

Chinese elm

- *hardy*
- *deciduous/ semi-evergreen*
- *easy to train*
- *corky bark*

Chinese elm is one of the most popular species to be used for bonsai and is an ideal plant for newcomers to the hobby. The species is variable and some forms, usually grown indoors, have smooth bark (see pages 310– 11). The plants with an attractive rough, corky bark are grown outdoors. The leaves are dark green, turning yellow or reddish in late autumn, and the small, red flowers in late summer are followed by green fruits.

There are many cultivars of Chinese elm to choose between, including *Ulmus parvifolia* 'Hokkaido' (which has especially small leaves and corky bark), *U.p.* 'Uzen', *U.p.* 'Catlin' and *U.p.* 'Nire', all of which are grown in Japan for bonsai. These trees are particularly suitable for the informal upright and broom styles.

Where to keep them

Although its common name is Chinese elm (zones 4– 5), this species is found in Japan and Korea as well as China. It is a hardy tree in temperate areas and needs no special protection in winter. It can be kept in full sun throughout the growing season. Note that some plants sold as

Chinese elm have smooth bark and are less hardy (zones 6– 9); these should be treated as indoor plants in some regions (see pages 310– 11).

Above: The wood of Chinese elm is very dense and hard. When left to weather naturally, the bark is extremely attractive.

How to look after them

REPOTTING: Repot Chinese elms every 2–3 years, in early spring. Use multi-purpose, free-draining compost consisting of equal parts loam, peat (or garden compost) and sharp sand.

PRUNING AND PINCHING: Regularly prune the twigs and branches, to create an attractive framework. If you have to remove a large branch, aim to do this in mid-summer, when calluses will form more readily. Pinch out the growing tips of the new shoots as they emerge, leaving two leaves. Continue to do this throughout the growing season.

WIRING: Wire heavy branches from time to time, to prevent them from curling upwards. Secondary and tertiary branches should also be wired, to encourage the formation of a good framework. The wires can be left on for a growing season.

WATERING: Water Chinese elms regularly from spring to autumn, increasing the amount in summer. Keep the compost moist in all seasons except winter, when it should be just moist.

FEEDING: Feed Chinese elm bonsai once a month, applying a high-nitrogen fertilizer in spring and then changing to a general one in mid-summer.

BE AWARE: Chinese elm is susceptible to leaf gall and aphids. Control leaf gall with an insecticidal spray. Aphids that cannot be removed by hand often respond better to systemic treatments. As far as is known, Chinese elm bonsai are not susceptible to Dutch elm disease.

Ulmus parvifolia

Zelkova serrata

Japanese grey-bark elm, Keyaki

- *hardy*
- *deciduous*
- *easy to train*
- *elegant*
- *vivid autumn colour*

These trees, which are closely related to *Ulmus* (see pages 164– 7), are among the most graceful amenity trees from Japan, where they are used extensively for street planting. Japanese grey-bark elm naturally develops a rather spreading habit. It has narrow, serrated, dark green leaves, which turn yellow-orange in autumn, and smooth, grey bark, which peels to reveal the orange tissue beneath. The natural habit is broom shaped, and bonsai are usually trained in the same style. Plants are available as bonsai from Japan, and those already trained are expensive.

Where to keep them

Japanese grey-bark elm (zone 5), which is native to South Korea, Japan and Taiwan, is hardy in temperate areas. It can be kept in full sun for most of the growing season, although it does best if given partial shade from strong, direct sunshine at the height of summer.

How to look after them

REPOTTING: Repot every 3– 4 years, in early spring. Use moisture-retentive but free-draining compost consisting

Above: The autumn colours of Japanese grey-bark elm range from yellow to scarlet, depending on the plant's exposure to sunlight and the fertilizer used.

of equal parts loam, peat (or garden compost) and sharp sand. Or try two parts loam to one part sharp sand.

PRUNING AND PINCHING: Japanese grey-bark elm bonsai benefit from leaf pruning (partial or total defoliation; see page 30) in early summer, to allow more sunlight into the twig structure. You should also remove any crossing branches (growing against the general direction of the other branches) at this time. During the growing season, pinch out the growing tips of new shoots as soon as two or three leaves emerge.

WIRING: Japanese grey-bark elm is shaped mainly through pruning. However, branches that require special training can be wired between spring and autumn.

WATERING: Water regularly throughout the growing season, providing more water in summer than in spring and autumn. Allow the surface of the compost to dry out a little between waterings, but never allow the compost to become completely dry or the leaves will wither and die. Keep the compost just moist in winter.

FEEDING: Apply a weak general fertilizer three or four times a year. Do not overfeed, as this will result in coarse growth and spoil the fine network of branches.

BE AWARE: Sometimes branches of Japanese grey-bark elm die back in winter. Remove the dead twigs in early spring, cutting back to healthy tissue. It is susceptible to infestations of scale insects, which are best treated by applying a systemic insecticide.

Zelkova serrata

169

Outdoor flowering BONSAI

Introduction

Most people are amazed to see flowering bonsai. They find it intriguing that a miniature tree can produce a crop of perfect flowers, which are often followed by full-sized fruit. It seems almost unbelievable that this should be possible on a delicate little tree. Yet this is within the grasp of even the most inexperienced bonsai growers. All flowering bonsai go through the natural cycle of growth, often beginning with foliage, followed by flowers and, finally, fruit.

Care of flowering bonsai

The plants in this group are no more difficult to grow as bonsai than they are as full-size flowering trees and shrubs. After all, a flowering bonsai is just a plant in a special pot, and most container-grown plants will continue to flower whether the pot they are in is shallow or deep. When pruning and pinching flowering bonsai, however, bear in mind that most species produce the next year's flowering buds on the current season's growth. For this reason, your flowering bonsai should usually not be pruned or pinched after mid-summer, or only very lightly.

Left: This pyracantha, in the root-over-rock style, has flowers in the spring, followed by scarlet berries in the autumn.

Flowering species

The flowers of some plants are gaudier than others. Most conifers and some deciduous species bear insignificant, scarcely noticeable flowers. Other plants, such as *Rhododendron indicum* (see pages 222–3) and wisterias (see pages 236–7), produce flamboyant, highly scented blooms.

The diversity of colour, shape and fragrance in flowering bonsai is amazing and is one of the reasons flowering bonsai are so popular. Their main disadvantage is that the flowering period is relatively short. Most of these plants bloom for just a couple of weeks, and when the flowers are over the plants are rarely as attractive. Plants that bear fruit, such as types of *Malus* (see pages 204–5), have the bonus of a slightly longer period of interest, as do plants such as *Chaenomeles japonica* (see pages 178–9), *Cotoneaster* (see pages 184–5), *Pseudocydonia sinensis* (see pages 218–19) and *Pyracantha angustifolia* (see pages 220–1). Others, such as *Camellia* (see pages 176–7), *Rhododendron indicum* and some species of *Elaeagnus* (see pages 190–1), are evergreen and look attractive whether or not they are in flower.

Above: These pink crab apple buds will develop into white or pale pink flowers.

Above: Satsuki azaleas bloom in early summer. Their bright flowers will provide a spectacular show for nearly a month.

A few hardy genera, such as *Crataegus* (see pages 186–9), *Potentilla* (see pages 210–11), *Prunus* (see pages 212–17), *Stewartia* (see pages 228–9) and *Styrax* (see pages 230–1), bear their flowers for longer than a few weeks.

Berberis

Berberis, Barberry

- *hardy, deciduous shrub*
- *lovely, autumn foliage*
- *easy to make into bonsai from nursery plants*

This is a large genus of more than 500 species of bushy plants growing mainly in northern temperate regions and some parts of South America. Some are evergreen, and some deciduous. They all bear flowers that are mostly small, followed by brightly coloured fruit. The stems are thorny – hence their popularity as hedging plants. Berberis also make excellent bonsai as they have interesting trunks as well as lovely foliage and flowers. *Berberis thunbergii* and *B. darwinii* are very popular with hobbyists, yet berberis bonsai are seldom grown for the commercial bonsai market.

Where to keep them

No protection is needed, as berberis (zones 4–8) are hardy plants. Keep them in full sun or semi-shade, although the leaves develop better autumn colours when grown in full sun.

How to look after them

REPOTTING: Repot once every other year, in spring, when pot bound. Use any free-draining compost.

Left: Most berberis species and cultivars bear interesting leaves, flowers and fruit. Autumn colours are spectacular.

PRUNING AND PINCHING: Prune heavily in spring and lightly throughout the growing season.

WIRING: Berberis can be wired at any time of year.

WATERING: Water regularly during the growing season.

FEEDING: Feed with a general fertilizer during the growing season; use a low nitrogen one in late summer.

BE AWARE: Aphids are fond of new, soft berberis growth. Remove them by jetting with a hose or applying insecticide.

Berberis thunbergii

Camellia

Camellia

- *hardy*
- *evergreen*
- *fairly easy to grow and train*
- *range of flower colours*

Camellias are among the most beautiful flowering shrubs to have been introduced to the West from China and Japan. Although they produce handsome, glossy, dark green leaves, they are grown for their lovely flowers, which vary in colour from white to deep red and in shape from single to formal double. The flowers are borne from winter to spring. Camellias with small leaves make excellent bonsai and are best grown in the informal upright style.

Where to keep them

Camellias (zones 6–8) are found in the wild in woodlands from northern India to China and Japan, and some species occur in Java and Indonesia. Most are hardy in temperate areas and, even when there is snow on the ground, flowers will still appear. However, you should move your bonsai to a frost-free place if prolonged periods with temperatures below -12°C (10°F) are forecast. If plants are outside in late winter or early spring, position them so early morning sun does not damage frosted buds. Heavy rain also harms delicate blooms. Camellias should be kept in partial shade in the growing season, as excessive sun will scorch the leaves.

How to look after them

REPOTTING: Repot camellias every 2–3 years, in early spring or immediately after flowering. Use acidic compost consisting of two parts loam, one part

Above: Camellias are grown as bonsai mainly for their exquisite flowers. Both the large- and small-flowered varieties are used.

peat (or garden compost) and one part sharp sand. (If they are put in alkaline compost, the leaves will turn yellow and the plants will die.)

PRUNING AND PINCHING: After deadheading to remove the spent flowers, prune back to one or two buds of the previous season's growth. Pinch out the growing tips of new shoots as they emerge, but do not pinch out after mid-summer in case you remove the shoots that will bear flowers the following spring.

WIRING: Use copper or aluminium wire, protected by raffia, to train branches that are up to a pencil thickness in width. The wire can be added at any time of the year except early spring. Wires can be kept on for a couple of years.

WATERING: Water regularly throughout the growing season, giving extra in summer. The compost must also be kept moist in winter, to avoid bud drop.

FEEDING: Immediately after flowering, apply a high-nitrogen fertilizer. Give a low-nitrogen feed later in summer.

BE AWARE: Camellias are especially susceptible to vine weevils. Check the compost thoroughly when repotting, and water nematodes into the compost in late spring. Aphids can also be a problem, and sooty mould sometimes develops in the honeydew they secrete. Apply a systemic insecticide and mist the leaves to clean them.

Camellia japonica

177

Chaenomeles japonica

Flowering quince

- *hardy*
- *deciduous*
- *easy to keep*
- *red, pink or white flowers*
- *fruit*

This plant is a member of the Rosaceae family. It has glossy, mid-green leaves and, in spring, clusters of red, pink or white flowers, which are followed by edible, yellow or yellow-flushed red fruits. Flowering quince is grown as bonsai mainly for its flowers. Its tendency to produce multiple stems means that it is normally grown in the clump style.

Where to keep them

Flowering quince (zones 4–6) is native to Japan and is perfectly hardy in temperate areas, needing no special winter protection. It thrives in full sun or partial shade throughout the growing season.

How to look after them

REPOTTING: Repot flowering quince every 2–3 years. This should be done in very early spring or immediately after flowering. In the temperate regions, it is also possible to repot in late autumn, provided the plant is protected from frost over winter. Use free-draining compost consisting of two parts loam, one part peat (or garden compost) and one part sharp sand.

Above: Flowering quince blooms in early spring. It is a welcome sight at a time when there is very little colour around.

PRUNING AND PINCHING: Prune back the old growth immediately after flowering and keep twigs and shoots trimmed to maintain the traditional bonsai shape. Do not prune too hard after mid-summer, or you will remove the next year's flowering shoots. The growing tips of new shoots can be pinched out as they emerge, but cease pinching out in late summer.

WIRING: Flowering quince does not need to be wired. The shape is achieved through pruning.

WATERING: Water flowering quince regularly throughout the growing season. Make sure that plants in small pots do not dry out in summer, and keep the compost just moist in winter.

FEEDING: After the plant has finished flowering in spring, feed flowering quince once with a high-nitrogen fertilizer. During mid- to late summer, feed it with a low-nitrogen fertilizer.

BE AWARE: All plants in the Rosaceae family are susceptible to rust and fireblight. Fireblight is especially serious.

Keep a close eye on the leaves for the symptoms – brown and black spots on the leaves or a whole branch turning brown for no reason – and prune and burn all affected parts. Sterilize your secateurs afterwards to avoid spreading the disease.

Chaenomeles japonica

Cornus

Cornel, Dogwood

- *hardy flowering shrub*
- *lovely, yellow flowers*
- *blooms early spring*
- *very easy to train and keep*

Cornus mas (cornelian cherry) and *C. officinalis* (Asiatic cornelian cherry) are deciduous shrubs or small trees that grow in cool temperate climates. They have bright yellow flowers borne on the bare stems in very early spring. The leaves are nondescript, although they do turn red in autumn. The small, ovoid fruit is edible and has many herbal and medicinal uses. The wood is extremely hard. Cornelian cherries are not often available as bonsai, although some Japanese growers do produce them. Fortunately, they are easy to make into bonsai from nursery plants, and they can be propagated from hardwood cuttings, layering or seeds.

Where to keep them

There is no need to protect cornelian cherry (zones 5–9) in winter as it is very hardy, but Asiatic cornelian cherry (zones 6–9) may need hard frost protection. Grow in full sun.

How to look after them

REPOTTING: Repot every 2–3 years, in late spring, after flowering, using free-draining, loamy soil.

Left: The flowers of the Asiatic cornelian cherry introduce a bright note to any spring day.

PRUNING AND PINCHING: Prune the plant immediately after flowering and trim again lightly in summer to create the desired shape. Do not prune heavily in late summer, or you will lose the flowering shoots.

WIRING: Cornelian cherry can be wired, in mid-summer, although the bonsai shape is easily achieved simply by pruning.

WATERING: Water regularly throughout the growing season. Keep the compost just moist in winter.

FEEDING: Feed after flowering with a low-nitrogen or rose fertilizer.

BE AWARE: Cornelian cherries are prone to scale and other insects. Treat the plants with an appropriate insecticide.

Cornus mas

Corylopsis spicata

Japanese witch hazel

- *hardy*
- *deciduous*
- *easy to grow and train*
- *fragrant, yellow flowers*

This is one of the most delightful shrubs discovered in Japan by the plant hunter Robert Fortune in the late 19th century. Bright yellow flowers appear in early spring on bare stems, like those of *Hamamelis* (witch hazel). The dark green leaves, slightly glaucous beneath, are oval. Japanese witch hazel is popular in Japan, but they are becoming more available in temperate countries. It is usually trained in informal or clump styles.

Above: It is not just the flowers of Japanese witch hazel that are attractive. When the petals drop, the sepals are still beautiful, too.

Where to keep them

Japanese witch hazel (zone 6) is a hardy species in temperate areas and requires no special protection in winter, although late spring frosts sometimes damage the flowers. It does best in partial shade during the growing season.

How to look after them

REPOTTING: In temperate climates, it is better to repot this plant in early spring, rather than immediately after flowering (as recommended by Japanese growers). It needs free-draining but moisture-retentive, lime-free (ericaceous) compost. Do not use alkaline compost, or the leaves will turn yellow and the plant will die.

PRUNING AND PINCHING: After flowering, deadhead Japanese witch hazel to remove the spent flowers, and prune the shoots to encourage new growth. The new branches will bear next year's crop of flowers, so be careful that you do not cut off all of these if you prune again during the summer. Pinch out the growing tips of new shoots as necessary, but do not pinch in late summer.

WIRING: If you wish to develop new branches, apply wires to new shoots so they do not spring upwards. Wire as soon as the shoots are hard, in mid-summer, and leave the wire for no more than two growing seasons.

WATERING: Water Japanese witch hazel regularly during the growing season, ensuring that the compost is never allowed to dry out. During the winter months, keep the compost just moist.

FEEDING: Apply a general fertilizer immediately after flowering. Plants also benefit from the application of a low-nitrogen fertilizer in late summer.

BE AWARE: Japanese witch hazel is an easy and enjoyable species to grow and is generally untroubled by pests and diseases.

Corylopsis spicata

183

Cotoneaster

Cotoneaster

- *hardy*
- *evergreen/deciduous*
- *easy to train*
- *tiny, white flowers*
- *orange or red berries*

Like many of the plants that are grown for their colourful berries, cotoneasters belong to the Rosaceae family. There are about 200 species in the genus, and many can be used for bonsai, but the two most popular are *Cotoneaster horizontalis* (herringbone cotoneaster), which is deciduous, and *C. integrifolius*, which is evergreen. Both species have small, delicate leaves, pinkish-white or white flowers and red berries, and they make attractive bonsai in the informal and cascade styles. Herringbone cotoneaster is particularly good for planting on rock, such as tufa, to make mountain scenes.

Above: Cotoneasters are grown mainly for their red or orange berries, although their flowers are also pretty and attract bees.

Cotoneasters are widely available in bonsai nurseries and are also popular with amateur enthusiasts for creating bonsai. They are extremely easy to propagate; young plants will grow very quickly and are ideal starter material for bonsai. Old shrubs dug from gardens are useful for larger specimen bonsai.

Where to keep them

Herringbone cotoneaster (zones 4–6) is native to western China, and *C. integrifolius* (zones 4–6) comes from the Himalayas. Both species are hardy in temperate areas, needing the protection of a frost-free shed or greenhouse only when prolonged spells of cold weather are forecast. Both species can be kept in full sun throughout the growing season.

Cotoneaster horizontalis

How to look after them

REPOTTING: Repot cotoneasters every other year. In Europe and North America, this is best done in late winter or early spring, not after flowering (as recommended in many Japanese books). Use free-draining, fertile compost consisting of two parts loam, one part leaf mould and one part sharp sand.

PRUNING AND PINCHING: Prune old growth in spring, before growth restarts. Throughout the growing season, cut back unwanted vigorous shoots as they appear. Pinch out the growing tips of new shoots as they emerge, but do not pinch after mid-summer, because you will remove the flowering shoots that produce the flowers for the next year.

WIRING: Wire the trunk and branches in spring, before the buds emerge. Protect soft branches with raffia. The wiring should be left on the branches for no more than one year or growing season.

WATERING: Water regularly. When plants are in flower, take care not to wet the flowers, which are easily damaged. Never allow smaller bonsai to dry out. Keep the compost just moist in winter.

FEEDING: Feed once after flowering in spring and again in early summer with a general fertilizer. Use a low-nitrogen fertilizer in late summer.

BE AWARE: Cotoneasters are prone to rust and fireblight. Fireblight is potentially serious; if you notice that shoots are turning black and leaves are withering, remove and burn all affected parts, and disinfect your secateurs.

Crataegus laevigata, syn. *C. oxyacantha*

Midland hawthorn, red hawthorn

- *hardy*
- *deciduous*
- *easy to train*
- *pink or red flowers*

Midland hawthorn is not as vigorous as *Crataegus monogyna* (see pages 188–9), but hardy nonetheless. Different varieties and cultivars bear single or double flowers and range in colour from pink to deep red. It does not set fruit as easily as *C. monogyna*. Many bonsai nurseries now stock Midland hawthorn, and bonsai can also readily be made from plants propagated at home.

Where to keep them

Midland hawthorn (zone 5) is native to Europe and eastwards to India, and it is hardy. Protect flower buds from late spring frosts. Although it can be kept in full sun throughout the growing season, it will benefit from being given some shade in very hot weather.

How to look after them

REPOTTING: Repot every 3–4 years in early spring. Midland hawthorn is not fussy about the type of soil, but it must be free draining, so use a mixture of two parts loam, one part peat (or garden compost) and one part sharp sand.

Above: The flowers of Midland hawthorn are really charming, rather like miniature posies. Pictured here is one of the double pink forms.

PRUNING AND PINCHING: After flowering, prune back old shoots to encourage the growth of new flowering ones. Take care to leave some of the old shoots if you want to encourage berries. Many new shoots will grow from the existing branches; these carry next year's flowering buds. Prune or pinch out the growing tips, as necessary, to maintain the shape, but avoid excessive pruning or pinching after mid-summer.

WIRING: New shoots can be wired from mid- to late summer. The wiring should not be left on for longer than one year.

WATERING: Water Midland hawthorn regularly, especially throughout the growing season. Do not allow the compost to dry out completely at any time, because this can lead to die-back. Be sure to keep the compost just moist during winter.

FEEDING: Apply a general fertilizer immediately after flowering, and follow this with a low-nitrogen feed in late summer.

BE AWARE: Because most Midland hawthorn plants are grafted, you must remove any suckers that develop from the roots as soon as you notice them.

This species is susceptible to rust and black spot (the same diseases that affect roses); spray with appropriate fungicides to provide effective control. It also tends to suffer from die-back of the crown, which may be due to insufficient water in summer or too shallow a pot. If die-back occurs, you can either use the dead branches as driftwood effects or cut them out completely and wait for new shoots to develop.

Crataegus laevigata

Crataegus monogyna

Common hedging hawthorn

- *hardy*
- *deciduous*
- *easy to train*
- *red, pink or white flowers*
- *red berries*

Common hedging hawthorn is hardy, vigorous and easy to train, and it bears abundant, red, pink or white flowers and red berries. Old plants with attractive, gnarled trunks can be found in hedgerows, and they make excellent bonsai specimens. Always seek permission from the landowner or local authority before collecting wild material. This is a favourite species with bonsai enthusiasts, and nurseries stock the plants as partly trained material and finished bonsai. The small, spiny trees are often used for garden hedging, and there are several cultivars.

Above: The red, pink or white flowers of common hedging hawthorn are followed by beautiful, red berries, which prolong the season of interest.

Where to keep them

Common hedging hawthorn (zone 4) is found throughout Europe. It is a vigorous, perfectly hardy species and does not need any protection in winter. Flower buds, however, should be sheltered from late spring frosts. It can be kept in full sun throughout the growing season.

How to look after them

REPOTTING: Repot every 3–4 years in early spring. It is not fussy about the type of soil, but it must be free draining, so use a mixture of two parts loam, one part peat (or garden compost) and one part sharp sand.

PRUNING AND PINCHING: After flowering, prune back some of the old shoots to encourage new growth, taking care to leave enough old shoots to produce a good crop of berries. Many new shoots will grow from the existing branches; these carry next year's flowering buds. Prune or pinch out the growing tips, as necessary, to maintain the shape of the tree, but avoid excessive pruning or pinching after mid-summer.

WIRING: New shoots can be wired from mid- to late summer. Wires should not be left on for longer than a year.

WATERING: Water regularly, especially throughout the growing season. Do not allow the compost to dry out, because this can lead to die-back. Keep the compost just moist in winter.

FEEDING: Apply a general fertilizer immediately after flowering, and follow this with a low-nitrogen feed in late summer.

BE AWARE: Common hedging hawthorn can be susceptible to mildew in wet summers. Treat by spraying with an appropriate fungicide.

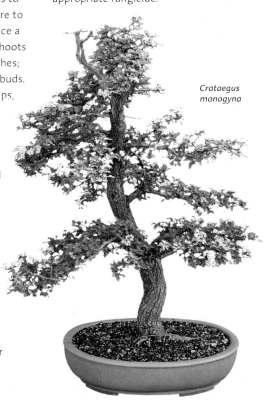

Crataegus monogyna

Elaeagnus

Elaeagnus

- *hardy*
- *deciduous/evergreen*
- *easy to keep*
- *fragrant flowers*
- *red fruit*

Two species of elaeagnus are commonly grown as bonsai. Both have dark green leaves, silvery beneath, and bear fragrant flowers in autumn, which are followed by fruits that ripen to red and persist until the following year. *Elaeagnus multiflora* (goumi) is a deciduous shrub, while *E. pungens* (silverthorn, thorny olive) is evergreen, and many cultivars have been developed from it. These plants are suitable for the informal upright style. They are popular for bonsai in Japan, where they are grown for their flowers and attractive fruit, but are less well known in other countries.

Where to keep them

Both goumi and silverthorn (both zones 4–7), which come from China and Japan, are completely hardy in temperate areas and need no special winter protection. In summer, they can be kept in full sun, and silverthorn in particular will lose the silvery sheen on its leaves if it is grown in shade.

How to look after them

REPOTTING: Repot goumi and silverthorn every 3–4 years in early spring. Use

Right: Goumi produces scented flowers in late spring. The flowers are followed by red fruit.

free-draining, fertile compost consisting of two parts loam, one part leaf mould and one part sharp sand.

PRUNING AND PINCHING: The aim of pruning these shrubs is to keep the internodes short. Both species are mostly pruned in summer, after flowering, when new shoots are cut back to maintain the overall framework of the bonsai. Pinch out the growing tips of new shoots as necessary, ensuring that you do not remove all of next year's flowering buds.

WIRING: Wire the main branches, because new shoots tend to grow upwards. Do this in mid-summer, when the new shoots have just hardened, and keep the wires on for one year or growing season.

WATERING: Water regularly throughout the growing season, allowing the surface of the compost to dry slightly before the next watering, although you should make sure that the rootball never dries out completely. Keep silverthorn moist in winter, and goumi only just moist.

FEEDING: These plants will appreciate the application of a high-nitrogen fertilizer in spring. Change to a low-nitrogen one in late summer. Do not feed in autumn or winter.

BE AWARE: Elaeagnus are susceptible to the fungal disease coral spot. Spray with an appropriate fungicide if you notice the symptoms. They are also often infested with scale insects, which can be treated with a systemic insecticide.

Elaeagnus pungens

Ficus carica

Common fig, Edible fig

- *Mediterranean fruit tree*
- *slightly tender*
- *attractive as bonsai*
- *easy to grow and keep*

This is one of the oldest cultivated fruit trees, believed to have been grown by humans for almost 5,000 years. It makes interesting bonsai, and is easy to train and grow. Gradually, common fig is becoming more available as bonsai from commercial nurseries, although bonsai hobbyists have been producing them for many years and they are very easy to propagate from cuttings. It is a vigorous plant but, if kept fairly pot bound, the leaves and fruit reduce in size.

Left: The fruit of common fig are both edible and beautiful. Birds also relish them.

Where to keep them

A native of the Mediterranean and Middle East, common fig (zones 6–11) thrives in hot, dry, semi-desert conditions. It has a fairly wide hardiness tolerance. Keep in full sun all year round if you live in a warm Mediterranean climate. During very hot summer days, some shade may prevent leaves from scorching. In cool temperate areas, grow in full sun during summer, and protect in a greenhouse or conservatory in winter.

How to look after them

REPOTTING: Repot every 2–3 years in spring. Any kind of soil can be used – figs thrive on poor soil.

PRUNING AND PINCHING: Pinch and prune often during the growing season to develop branching. This also encourages reduction in leaf size.

WIRING: There is no need to wire, because shapes can be achieved simply by pruning.

WATERING: Water this drought-resistant plant sparingly. Excessive watering results in large leaves and long internodes.

FEEDING: Feed sparingly, enough to keep foliage green, with a general fertilizer in spring. Use a high-potash one in late summer to encourage fruiting.

BE AWARE: Net the plant before birds take the fruit.

Ficus carica

Forsythia

Forsythia

- *hardy*
- *deciduous*
- *easy to keep*
- *yellow flowers*

Forsythias are among the most colourful of the early flowering shrubs, and they are common garden plants, with their familiar, yellow flowers appearing on bare stems in spring. Both *Forsythia* x *intermedia* and *F. suspensa* (golden bell) are used as bonsai in Japan and are suitable for the informal, cascade and root-over-rock styles. They are sometimes available in bonsai nurseries. Large trunk specimens can also be made from established garden plants. Choose one with interest in the roots or trunk and trim it back as desired. New shoots will grow from the old wood and can be wired when hard.

Where to keep them

Forsythias (zone 4) are hardy plants in temperate areas, and they need no special winter protection. Keep these plants in full sun throughout the year.

How to look after them

REPOTTING: Repot every other year, in early spring, into free-draining, fertile compost comprising equal parts loam, peat (or garden compost) and sharp sand.

Right: Trim back forsythia's long, new shoots in mid-summer, to encourage sideshoots to develop (as shown here). These shoots will carry the next year's flowers.

PRUNING AND PINCHING: Prune the old shoots that carried the current season's flowers immediately after flowering to encourage new flowering shoots to grow. Shorten any long new shoots, to keep the plant in shape and stimulate the production of secondary branches. Pinch out the growing tips of these when two or three leaves have formed, but avoid excessive pinching after mid-summer, to ensure you do not remove the following year's flowering buds.

WIRING: Do not wire forsythia if you are happy with the existing shape. If you need to wire any branches growing in the wrong direction, leave the wires on for only a year.

WATERING: Water forsythia regularly throughout the growing season. Make sure that the compost is not allowed to dry out completely, especially during autumn, when the flower buds are forming for the next year. Keep the compost just moist in winter.

FEEDING: Apply a general fertilizer after flowering. Plants will also benefit from a low-nitrogen feed in late summer.

BE AWARE: Aphids are sometimes a problem, but usually in such limited numbers that they can be removed by hand. Forsythias are not long-lived as bonsai, because their trunks tend to rot with age. When the rot has extended too far to be rescued, it is best to start again with a young plant.

Forsythia x intermedia

Hydrangea anomala subsp. *petiolaris*

Climbing hydrangea

- *unusual but attractive bonsai*
- *hardy*
- *easy to care for*
- *lacecap flowers*

Many of the climbing hydrangea, such as this one, are suitable for bonsai as they have woody trunks. It grows wild in Japan and Korea and is ideal for making bonsai. It produces dainty, heart-shaped leaves and beautiful lacecap flowers in pink or white. In Japan, climbing hydrangea bonsai is highly prized because it is unusual, and good specimens are always a talking point. Old plants from gardens or nurseries are a good source of raw material of climbing hydrangea, which is not difficult to make into bonsai. The most popular style is cascade, although it makes an attractive informal upright tree too.

Where to keep them
Climbing hydrangea (zones 4–8) is hardy. As it is a woodland plant, it prefers shade but can be grown in sun.

How to look after them
REPOTTING: Repot every 2–3 years in spring. Use loam-based compost consisting of two parts loam, one part leaf mould (garden compost or peat) and one part sand.

Right: The flowers of climbing hydrangea are similar to those of lacecap ones.

PRUNING AND PINCHING: Prune back in mid-summer after flowering. Do not do this in autumn or spring, as you could be removing the flowering shoots.

WIRING: There is no need to wire unless you have to create a special shape.

WATERING: Keep well watered in the growing season; do not let the soil dry out. In winter, the soil should be damp, but not waterlogged.

FEEDING: Feed with a general fertilizer during spring and summer.

BE AWARE: Look out for the pests such as aphids, leaf miners and vine weevil. Treat by jetting off with a hose or applying an appropriate insecticide.

Hydrangea anomala subsp. *petiolaris*

Ilex serrata

Japanese holly, Japanese winterberry

- *half-hardy*
- *deciduous*
- *challenging as a bonsai plant*
- *bright red berries*

This deciduous holly is grown for its bright red berries. It has small, oval, pointed leaves, which turn slightly yellow in autumn. Male and female flowers are borne on separate plants, so it is important to distinguish between the sexes when buying a plant. For fruit to set, plants of both sexes are needed for effective pollination. Japanese holly is a popular bonsai in Japan, and fine specimens are in the informal style, with tapering trunks and a good root base. They are occasionally available from nurseries that import bonsai from Japan. This is not a plant for beginners.

Where to keep them

The species (zones 7–8) is native to Japan and China, but it is not hardy and requires protection in a frost-free greenhouse or shed in winter and spring. Keep in full sun in summer and autumn.

How to look after them

REPOTTING: Repot Japanese holly every 2–3 years, during early spring. Use

Left: The tiny red berries of Japanese holly are delightful. They remain on the plant after all the leaves have been shed.

moisture-retentive but free-draining compost consisting of equal parts loam, peat (or garden compost) and sharp sand.

PRUNING AND PINCHING: Prune any long new shoots in early summer and prune again very lightly in autumn to maintain the plant's overall shape. The next year's flowers are borne on the current season's shoots, so take care not to remove all the potential flowers. Pinch out some of the new buds as they form, but leave others until the foliage has hardened.

WIRING: Wire branches in mid-summer. The wires should not be left on for longer than a year.

WATERING: It is crucial that these plants are watered regularly throughout the growing season. If the rootball is allowed to dry out, even briefly, the tree will die. Keep the compost just moist in winter.

FEEDING: Apply a general fertilizer after the fruits have set. Plants will benefit from a low-nitrogen fertilizer in late summer.

BE AWARE: Aphids sometimes attack young shoots but can usually be controlled by hand. Use a systemic insecticide if the problem persists.

As Japanese holly is grown mainly for its attractive berries, check with nursery staff that the tree you are buying is indeed a female. You will also need to source a male plant for pollination. If you cannot obtain a male tree, then the next best thing is to place your bonsai in close proximity to *Ilex aquifolium* (see pages 142–3). There is a good chance that this will lead to a successful pollination.

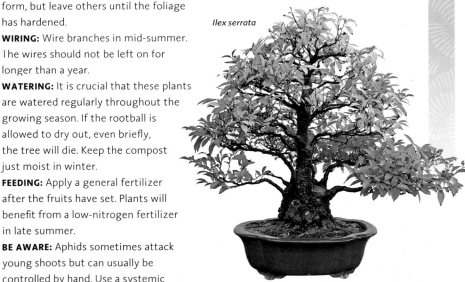

Ilex serrata

Jasminum nudiflorum

Winter jasmine

- hardy
- deciduous
- easy to keep
- yellow, winter flowers

This is one of the few shrubs to flower in the middle of winter. The yellow blooms appear on the bare stems in late autumn and sometimes continue right through to late winter or early spring. Although the young stems are rather lax and garden-grown plants are usually trained against a trellis or along wires, the mature stems of winter jasmine are thick and have a tree-like appearance, which makes them suitable for bonsai. Plants can be trained in the informal and cascade styles, and are popular in Japan as *shohin* (small) and *mame* (miniature) bonsai. They are available from commercial bonsai nurseries.

Where to keep them

Winter jasmine (zones 3–4), which comes originally from western China, is completely hardy, so winter protection is unnecessary. Keep it in full sun throughout the growing season.

How to look after them

REPOTTING: Winter jasmine is one of the few species that is best repotted after flowering. It is a fairly slow-growing plant, and repotting every other year in early spring, after the winter flowering, will be sufficient. Use loam-based

Left: The leaves of winter jasmine are divided into three long, oval leaflets. The flowers appear in the leaf axils along the bare stems.

compost consisting of two parts loam, one part leaf mould (garden compost or peat) and one part sand. Fine Akadama is a good substitute for loam.

PRUNING AND PINCHING: Prune the shoots that carried the current season's flowers immediately after flowering to encourage new ones to grow. Shorten new shoots once they have reached the desired length to stimulate the production of secondary branches and, if required, to make them look more rigid and branch-like. Pinch out the growing tips of the secondary growth when three or four leaves have formed to encourage flowering buds to develop. In late summer, take care not to remove such buds.

WIRING: If necessary, wire from spring to summer, protecting the delicate stems with raffia.

WATERING: Water freely throughout the growing season, taking particular care that the compost does not dry out in autumn, when the flower buds will be forming for next year. Keep the compost moist in winter.

FEEDING: Apply a general fertilizer to winter jasmine in mid-summer, 4–6 weeks after repotting. Apply a low-nitrogen fertilizer in early autumn.

BE AWARE: Vine weevils can be a problem. Check the compost when you repot, and water nematodes into the soil in late spring. Aphids sometimes attack young shoots, but can usually be removed by hand. Use a systemic insecticide if the problem persists.

Jasminum nudiflorum

Lespedeza bicolor

Japanese bush clover

- *beautiful mauve flowers*
- *hardy shrub*
- *easy to make into bonsai*
- *simple to keep*

There are many species of bush clover, which is a member of the pea family. Some are native to North America and Australia, but the majority originate from China, Korea and Japan. The cultivated varieties have beautiful, rose-pink or purple flowers. Japanese bush clover is a deciduous shrub, which grows wild on the hillsides of Japan. It flowers in late summer, when very little else is in bloom, and is very popular as a pot plant in Japan. As a bonsai, the flowers are considered more important than the shape of the tree, which is easy to make into bonsai from nursery stock.

Where to keep them

Japanese bush clover (zones 4–8) is hardy in temperate regions. It grows in full sun or semi-shade.

How to look after them

REPOTTING: Repot every other year, in spring, with compost (at least half of which should be loam), or use medium to fine Akadama.

PRUNING AND PINCHING: Japanese bush clover flowers on the current season's

Left: Japanese bush clover generally has purple flowers, but the new cultivars produce pink and white ones.

wood, so prune back hard in early spring. If you prune again immediately after its late summer flowering, you might get a second crop of flowers in late autumn.

WIRING: No need to wire, because the plant is grown mainly for its flowers.

WATERING: Apply a lot of water especially when it is in blossom. Be careful not to let the soil dry out, as the leaves will shrivel.

FEEDING: Feed with a general fertilizer from mid- to late summer. Japanese bush clover does not need a high-nitrogen feed, because the roots of this leguminous plant release nitrogen into the soil.

BE AWARE: Aphids and fluffy scale insects are attracted to Japanese bush clover. Treat any infestation with insecticide.

Lespedeza bicolor

Malus

Crab apple, Hime ringo

- *hardy*
- *deciduous*
- *easy to keep*
- *pretty flowers*
- *colourful autumn fruit*

Many species of *Malus* can be used for bonsai, and the most popular ones include *M. baccata* (Siberian crab apple), *M. floribunda* (Japanese crab apple), *M. halliana* (Hall's crab apple) and *M.* x *micromalus* (Makino, Kaido crab apple). They are grown for their attractive flowers and their delightful, small fruit, which are the right scale for the bonsai. These plants are either self-pollinating or they can pollinate other crab apples nearby.

Crab apples are suitable for most bonsai styles except windswept, driftwood, forest and literati. They are popular as bonsai in Japan, but many species and varieties cannot be imported to many countries in the world. They can, however, be grown easily from seed.

Where to keep them

These hardy plants (zones 4–6) need no special protection in winter and can be kept in full sun throughout the growing season.

How to look after them

REPOTTING: Repot crab apples every other year, in early spring. Use multi-purpose, free-draining compost or one that consists of equal parts loam and sharp sand.

PRUNING AND PINCHING: Prune crab apples in late summer, after the new shoots have formed, cutting back to

Left: Crab apple flowers are available in many colours, ranging from pale pink fading to white, to dark pink or deep red.

two or three nodes or leaves. Pinch out the growing tips of the secondary shoots to channel the energy of the bonsai into flower-bud production and keep the plant looking trim. Be careful not to remove or pinch off next year's flower buds, which are usually formed in mid-summer.

WIRING: If you feel it is necessary to wire your crab apple bonsai, apply the wires any time from spring to autumn. You may need to use raffia under the wires to protect the bark from damage.

WATERING: Water crab apples regularly throughout the growing season. Take special care during summer to ensure that the compost does not dry out. In winter, keep the compost just moist.

FEEDING: Apply a general fertilizer, after the fruits have set, in mid-summer. Encourage flower buds to form by feeding the plant in late summer with a low-nitrogen fertilizer. Never fertilize immediately after flowering, because this will cause the newly set fruit to drop.

BE AWARE: Crab apples are susceptible to infestations of aphids, which can be treated with a systemic insecticide or picked off by hand. They are also prone to rust and canker; spray with an appropriate fungicide. If mildew occurs, improve the ventilation by standing the tree in a more open environment and spray with an appropriate fungicide. Always burn infected leaves.

Malus baccata

Morus

Mulberry

- *hardy*
- *deciduous*
- *easy to keep and train*
- *pink and red fruit*

Morus alba (white mulberry), *M. nigra* (black mulberry) and *M. rubra* (red mulberry) are grown mainly for their fruits. White mulberry is a spreading tree with glossy, bright green leaves and white fruits, which ripen to pink and red. Black mulberry is more rounded in habit, with mid-green leaves and rather acidic fruits, while red mulberry has sweet-tasting fruit ripening to dark purple. These species are especially good for bonsai, as the leaves and fruit reduce in size when the trees are grown in pots. They are suitable for the informal upright style with a thick trunk (the trunks on old specimens are rugged and full of character). Mulberries are available as bonsai in nurseries.

Where to keep them

White mulberry is native to China, and black mulberry is believed to have come originally from south-western Asia, while red mulberry is native to eastern North America. All are hardy in temperate areas (zones 6– 7), but need protecting from hard frosts in winter because their fleshy roots can rot. To thrive, these bonsai should be kept in full sun throughout the growing season.

How to look after them

REPOTTING: Repot every other year, during early spring. Use free-draining but moisture-retentive compost

Left: Mulberry flowers are insignificant, but the colourful fruits are certainly attractive and even edible, though rather small in size.

consisting of equal parts loam, peat (or garden compost) and sharp sand.

PRUNING AND PINCHING: Prune for shape in early spring, and again after flowering, from mid- to late summer, when the shoots have grown too long. Pruning and pinching back to two or three new leaves will keep the tree in shape and encourage new shoots. Take care not to remove all the year's flowering buds, which are formed during the previous growing season. Some of the old shoots that bore the current year's fruit should also be cut off, to encourage new ones to grow. If you want to create driftwood effects by hollowing out the thick trunk (see page 33), do so during spring and summer when the tree is in vigorous growth and will recover quickly.

WIRING: Wire the branches of larger mulberry specimens. Small trees that have short branches need not be wired. Put on the wire when the new shoots have hardened, in mid-summer. Retain it in position until the end of the growing season.

WATERING: Water mulberries regularly throughout the growing season, especially during summer. Keep the compost just moist throughout winter.

FEEDING: Apply a general fertilizer in mid-summer, and a low-nitrogen one in late summer.

BE AWARE: Caterpillars can defoliate mulberry plants. Pick off these pests by hand as soon as you notice them. Aphids can also be removed by hand or with a jet of water, or they can be treated with a systemic insecticide if they become a problem. Fungicidal sprays may be needed to combat coral spot and canker.

Morus rubra 'Nana'

207

Myrtus communis

Common myrtle

- *evergreen Mediterranean shrub*
- *aromatic*
- *attractive flowers*
- *protect from frosts*

This evergreen shrub – a native of the Mediterranean region – has aromatic leaves and beautiful white flowers, which are slightly scented. The flowers are followed by tiny, purple-black berries. Common myrtle is a medicinal plant, with many herbal properties, and is also used for making wines and liqueurs. It is easy to propagate from cuttings.

Where to keep them

Common myrtle (zones 5– 10) flourishes in Mediterranean, subtropical and tropical climates. It tolerates only -5°C (23°F), so in temperate regions provide winter protection from hard frost by moving it into a conservatory or indoor windowsill. When grown indoors, it needs lots of light and fresh air, and protection from drafts and frost. In warm climates, keep it in full sun.

How to look after them

REPOTTING: Repot every other year, in spring, using compost consisting of loam, organic matter and sharp sand.

Left: The scented white flowers of common myrtle have these lovely long stamens. New foliage is tinged red.

PRUNING AND PINCHING: Prune to maintain the shape of the tree. Be careful not to prune too much in summer, as there is a danger of cutting off the flowering shoots.

WIRING: Common myrtle can be wired at any time, but pruning is usually sufficient to keep the tree looking good.

WATERING: Water regularly, and do not let the soil dry out.

FEEDING: Feed the plant with a general fertilizer during the growing season.

BE AWARE: Common myrtle is prone to pests such as scale insects and aphids; treat with insecticide. Use an appropriate chemical to control vine weevil, or introduce predatory nematodes, which destroy the grubs in the soil.

Myrtus communis

Potentilla fruticosa

Potentilla, Cinquefoil

- hardy
- deciduous
- easy to keep
- range of flower colours
- flaky bark

This popular garden shrub has small leaves and lovely, yellow, saucer-shaped flowers, which appear throughout summer on the current season's shoots. Many cultivars with different coloured flowers have been developed. This species makes excellent bonsai with either slender or thick trunks, and the flaking bark creates added interest. Potentilla is extremely popular as bonsai in Japan, and older specimens are valuable. It is suitable for the informal upright, cascade and literati styles, and is widely available from bonsai nurseries.

Where to keep them

Potentilla (zones 2–8) is found in Europe, northern Asia and North America, and it is hardy in temperate areas. It requires no special protection in winter and can be kept in full sun throughout the growing season.

How to look after them

REPOTTING: Repot every other year, during early spring. Use multi-purpose, free-draining compost consisting of

Right: Like buttercups, potentilla flowers always look fresh and lovely. Deadheading spent flowers will encourage a continuous crop during summer.

one part loam, one part peat (or garden compost) and two parts sharp sand.

PRUNING AND PINCHING: After flowering has finished, in late summer, prune back long shoots. Pinch out the growing tips of the secondary shoots when two or three new leaves have emerged, to stimulate new flowering shoots. New shoots on the secondary branches will bear next year's crop of flowers, so just trim these lightly in late summer.

WIRING: Potentilla does not need much wiring. If required, wire hardened shoots in late summer.

WATERING: Water regularly during the growing season. Keep the compost just moist in winter.

FEEDING: Apply a general fertilizer once a month from spring to late summer.

BE AWARE: Potentilla is relatively trouble free and has a reputation for being difficult to kill.

Potentilla fruticosa

211

Prunus

Ornamental cherry

- *variable hardiness*
- *deciduous*
- *pretty flowers*
- *autumn fruits*

This is a very large genus, which includes *Prunus armeniaca* (apricot), *P. cerasifera* (cherry plum), *P. incisa* (Fuji cherry), *P. mume* (Japanese apricot), *P. persica* (peach), *P. serrulata* (oriental cherry), *P. spinosa* (blackthorn, sloe), *P.* x *subhirtella* 'Autumnalis', *P. tomentosa* (downy cherry, Nanking cherry) and *P.* x *yedoensis* (Yoshino cherry). Most are spring-flowering trees, but *P.* x *subhirtella* blooms from late autumn to early spring, and Japanese apricot bears highly scented flowers from late winter to early spring. They all make excellent bonsai, but Japanese apricot is the most highly prized.

Above: Cherry blossom is very attractive but short-lived – lasting only a few days. Many species and cultivars can be used for bonsai.

All these species are suitable for most styles, including windswept and literati, because old specimens have gnarled and twisted trunks. Unfortunately, many countries prohibit the importation of this genus, and so it is seldom seen outside Japan, where you are almost certain to find one among the best exhibits at major bonsai shows.

Where to keep them

Most of these ornamental trees are completely hardy (zones 4–6) and require no special protection in winter. However, apricot, Japanese apricot and peach are not reliably hardy (zones 8–9) and should be moved to a frost-free greenhouse or shed in winter. All ornamental cherries can be kept in full sun throughout the growing season.

How to look after them

REPOTTING: Repot every other year, in early spring, into free-draining compost consisting of two parts loam and one of sharp sand to which has been added a little bonemeal and a sprinkling of lime.

PRUNING AND PINCHING: Prune immediately after flowering to encourage new growth. Lightly cut back or pinch out the growing tips of the long shoots in early autumn. Avoid pruning or pinching out during summer, as this is when the flowering shoots for the following year develop.

WIRING: Wire from spring to summer, taking care not to damage the bark or knock off developing flower buds. Wires can be left on for a year.

WATERING: Water regularly in the growing season, especially in summer. Take care not to splash the petals, which are easily damaged by water. Keep the compost just moist in winter.

FEEDING: Apply a general fertilizer in spring, and a low-nitrogen one in late summer. Because most plants in this genus bear stoned fruit, they benefit from a fertilizer with a high calcium content.

BE AWARE: These plants are susceptible to rust; spray with an appropriate fungicide if you notice any symptoms. Aphids can be removed by hand, or treated with a systemic insecticide. Pick off caterpillars by hand.

Prunus incisa

Prunus spinosa

Blackthorn, Sloe

- hardy
- easy to look after
- edible fruit
- dense wood
- sharp thorns

This thorny shrub grows wild in hedgerows throughout Europe and west Asia. Its dark purple edible fruit has many culinary uses and is also made into wines and spirits. Blackthorn bears lovely white flowers, which appear in early spring before the leaves emerge. Its habit is very similar of *Prunus mume* (Japanese apricot), although blackthorn is much hardier. The wood is extremely dense, and the thorns on the branches are very sharp. Although it makes beautiful bonsai and is very popular with hobbyists, blackthorn is not often available in bonsai nurseries. Young plants are obtainable from general nurseries, but good examples of bonsai are usually made from plants collected from hedgerows or from the wild.

Where to keep them

Although blackthorn (zones 3–6) is frost hardy, when grown as bonsai it may not be able to tolerate hard frost (-5°C/23°F, or lower). Grow in full sun in summer.

How to look after them

REPOTTING: Repot every 2–3 years or when tree becomes pot bound. Do this immediately after flowering, that is mid-spring. Any free-draining compost is suitable.

Above: Most plants of the *Prunus* genus have attractive flowers and fruit. Blackthorn (shown here) is no exception.

PRUNING AND PINCHING: This vigorous grower needs cutting back especially in the early part of the growing season. Use pruning shears, rather than finger pinching, as blackthorn is a thorny plant. Cut out any inward-pointing shoots to maintain good branch structure. Prune sparingly after mid-summer, because you could be removing next year's flowering shoots.

WIRING: Blackthorn is a difficult species to wire, as the branches have sharp spines. Wire if you have to, but a good bonsai shape can be achieved simply by pruning.

WATERING: Water regularly in the growing season, especially in summer – do not let the soil dry out completely. Keep the compost just moist in winter.

FEEDING: As with most flowering plants, feed immediately after flowering, using a general fertilizer in early summer; then apply a low-nitrogen one in late summer.

BE AWARE: Watch out for aphids and scale insects; blast them off with a jet of water or use an insecticide. As all *Prunus* species belong to the Rosaceae family, they are prone to fireblight, so, if a branch suddenly withers and dies,

promptly cut it out and burn it, to reduce the spread of the disease.

Prunus spinosa

215

Prunus tomentosa

Downy cherry, Nanking cherry

- *hardy flowering and fruiting shrub*
- *attractive fruit and foliage*
- *one of the best* Prunus *species for bonsai*

Downy cherry, from western China, has been cultivated for centuries. It has downy leaves with good autumn colour, and its profuse, pinkish white flowers are single or sometimes double. The fruit is edible, small and bright red when ripe. It has many uses such as for making wine, juice or jam.

Where to keep them

Grow this hardy plant (zones 3–10) in full sun but move to partial shade in mid-summer, to prevent leaves from scorching.

How to look after them

REPOTTING: Repot every other year, in early spring, with loamy, free-draining compost consisting of equal parts loam, humus and sharp sand.

PRUNING AND PINCHING: Prune in late spring after flowering. Do not prune in late summer, as you could cut off the flowering shoots for next year.

WIRING: Downy cherry can be wired in mid-summer, although pruning will achieve the desired shape.

WATERING: Keep well watered during the growing season, but allow to dry between watering.

FEEDING: Feed with a high-nitrogen fertilizer after flowering, and with a low-nitrogen one in mid- and late summer.

BE AWARE: Scale insects can be a problem; control them with insecticide.

Above: In mid-summer, the fruit of downy cherry are red and its foliage deep green. In autumn, the leaves turn crimson.

Prunus tomentosa

Pseudocydonia sinensis, syn. *Cydonia sinensis*

Chinese quince

- *half-hardy*
- *deciduous*
- *quite challenging*
- *pink flowers*
- *unusual fruit*

This member of the Rosaceae family is closely related to *Chaenomeles japonica* (see pages 178–9). It has large leaves, which turn rich orange in autumn. The flowers appear in early spring and are a delightful shade of pink, while the large fruits are oval and turn golden-yellow as they ripen. The bark flakes and peels attractively. This is not among the easiest of bonsai to keep. It is suitable only for the informal and formal upright styles. Some countries prohibit the importation of Chinese quince, so plants may not be easily available.

Above: The large edible fruits of Chinese quince stay on the tree for a long time. At bonsai shows in Japan, they are always a talking point.

Where to keep them

Chinese quince (zones 6–7), which is native to China, is not reliably hardy and needs some protection in winter. Place your plant in an unheated greenhouse, or a heated greenhouse if the temperature is likely to fall below -5°C (23°F). It can be kept in full sun throughout the growing season.

How to look after them

REPOTTING: Repot Chinese quince every other year. The best time to do this is during early spring. Use free-draining compost consisting of two parts loam, one part peat (or garden compost) and one part sharp sand.

PRUNING AND PINCHING: New shoots will grow immediately after flowering. Leave these to extend until mid-summer, and then cut off their tips to stimulate the growth of secondary shoots. In late summer, pinch out the growing tips of the secondary growths, when two or three new leaves have emerged. The new shoots will bear next year's crop of flowers, so do not remove all the buds. The quinces are borne on old shoots that flowered in the current season.

WIRING: The best time to wire the branches is in mid-summer. The wires can be left on for a year.

WATERING: Water regularly and generously throughout the growing season, and never let the soil around the rootball dry out. Keep the soil just moist in winter.

FEEDING: Feed only after the fruit has set. If you feed too early, the young quinces will drop off. Apply a general fertilizer in early summer and follow this with a low-nitrogen one in late summer.

BE AWARE: Scale insects can be a problem and are best treated with a

Pseudocydonia sinensis

systemic insecticide. Look out for vine weevil larvae when you are repotting. Kill any that you find, and water nematodes into the compost during late spring.

219

Pyracantha angustifolia

Firethorn

- *half-hardy*
- *evergreen*
- *easy to train*
- *white flowers*
- *red berries*

The genus *Pyracantha* resembles the genus *Cotoneaster* (see pages 184– 5) in many respects except that it has sharp thorns. The species *P. angustifolia* is an evergreen shrub, often used for hedging in the garden. It produces clusters of lovely, white, five-petalled flowers in early summer, and these are followed by bright red berries in autumn. It easily develops a thick trunk and is an excellent subject for bonsai, being used for most styles.

Above: Firethorn flowers profusely in late spring, and the flowers are followed by an abundance of brightly coloured berries in autumn.

Where to keep them

Firethorn (zones 6– 8), which is originally from western China, is not reliably hardy and requires protection from hard frosts in the winter months. Keep your plant in an unheated greenhouse, or a heated greenhouse if the temperature is likely to fall below -5°C (23°F). Firethorn loses its leaves in very cold weather. It enjoys full sun throughout the growing season.

How to look after them

REPOTTING: Repot firethorn in early spring. It is a vigorous plant and should be repotted every other year. Use free-draining compost consisting of two parts loam, one part peat (or garden compost) and one part sharp sand.

PRUNING AND PINCHING: This is a thorny shrub and needs to be pruned with scissors, to maintain the overall shape of the tree, rather than pinched with fingers. Prune back the new shoots that grow after flowering in mid-summer. Trim again before winter, removing dead shoots and pruning out a few of the old flowering shoots to encourage new lateral shoots to develop. Take care not to remove all of the next year's buds.

WIRING: Firethorn is best wired in late autumn or early spring. The wires can be left on for a year.

WATERING: Water firethorn throughout the year. This includes dry spells in winter, although it needs more water in summer than in winter. Do not let the tree dry out during summer, because this will make the leaves wither and fall.

FEEDING: Start feeding only after flowering. Begin by applying a high-nitrogen fertilizer in mid-summer, followed by a low-nitrogen feed in late summer.

BE AWARE: Coral spot and scab may cause problems, but fireblight, which affects members of the Rosaceae family, is the most serious problem. Infected shoots must be removed and burned, and you should disinfect your secateurs. Aphids can be picked off by hand, removed with a jet of water or treated with a systemic insecticide if the infestation persists. Caterpillars are best removed by hand.

Pyracantha angustifolia

Rhododendron indicum

Satsuki azalea

- *half-hardy*
- *evergreen*
- *easy to keep and train*
- *range of flower colours*

Satsuki azaleas, which have been developed from *Rhododendron simsii* and *R. indicum*, are probably the most popular flowering bonsai in Japan, and there are specialist societies dedicated to the plant. Satsukis flower in the fifth month of the oriental calendar (early June in Japan), and the flowers can last for up to a month. The flowers are showy, and are often multicoloured on the same plant. A satsuki azalea in full bloom is a wonderful sight. This plant is usually trained in the informal upright style. It is readily available from bonsai nurseries.

Where to keep them

Satsuki azalea (zones 6–8) is hardy in mild temperate climates, where it needs no winter protection. It tolerates temperatures as low as -7°C (20°F) for short periods, and an open shade structure is adequate protection. Where temperatures fall below -7°C (20°F) for prolonged periods, protect in an unheated or moderately heated greenhouse. In the growing season, it can be kept in full sun or semi-shade; the latter will result in better leaf colour.

How to look after them

REPOTTING: Repot satsuki every 3–4 years. Japanese growers do this immediately after flowering, at the

Left: Many satsuki azaleas bear flowers of more than one colour on the same tree. Identifying a particular variety correctly can be difficult, because many are very similar.

start of the rainy season. In temperate countries, repotting in early spring, before flowering, is a better option. Always use Japanese Kanuma soil, with 30 per cent sphagnum moss peat.

PRUNING AND PINCHING: Japanese growers sometimes prune hard in early spring, sacrificing the season's crop of flowers to produce a better framework. Deadhead immediately after flowering Pruning can also be done at this time, before the leaves have hardened. Cut back secondary shoots to two pairs of leaves. When you repot, remove any dead or overcrowded branches. Satsuki azalea is not usually pinched.

WIRING: Wiring is best left until autumn or winter. The wires can remain for a year.

WATERING: Water regularly and generously throughout the year, but especially when the plants are in bloom. The petals are easily damaged, so take care not to splash them with water. Japanese growers keep satsuki azalea under cover when in flower to protect the blooms. Keep the compost just moist in winter.

FEEDING: Apply a fairly weak fertilizer immediately after flowering and again

Rhododendron indicum 'Hikari-no-tsukasa'

in autumn. Japanese growers like to use a rapeseed fertilizer.

BE AWARE: Kill any vine weevils and water nematodes into the soil in late spring. Spray leaf hoppers and rhododendron bugs with an appropriate insecticide. Pick off and burn foliage affected by azalea leaf gall. Aphids can usually be removed by hand.

223

Rosa

Rose

- *hardy*
- *colourful flowers*
- *easy to grow*
- *anyone can make a rose bonsai*

Roses grow all over the world, and they make lovely bonsai, being hardy, colourful and easy to grow. Some bonsai nurseries produce them as bonsai using hybrid 'miniature' varieties or species roses that bear small flowers, but any hobbyist with a bit of imagination can make lovely bonsai from nursery or garden stock. Attractive specimens can be created from old garden plants that have interesting, thick trunks.

Above: Miniature roses, such as in this Japanese bonsai nursery, are attractive plants.

Where to keep them

The wild rose species are usually frost hardy (zones 4–10), but some protection from frost may be necessary depending on the variety used. Place in full sun or partial shade in summer.

How to look after them

REPOTTING: Repot rose bonsai every other year, in the spring. Make sure that you use free-draining compost consisting of equal parts loam, humus and sharp sand.

PRUNING AND PINCHING: Prune in late winter to encourage new flowering shoots to develop. Do not prune or pinch in mid-summer, because you will remove the flowering shoots.

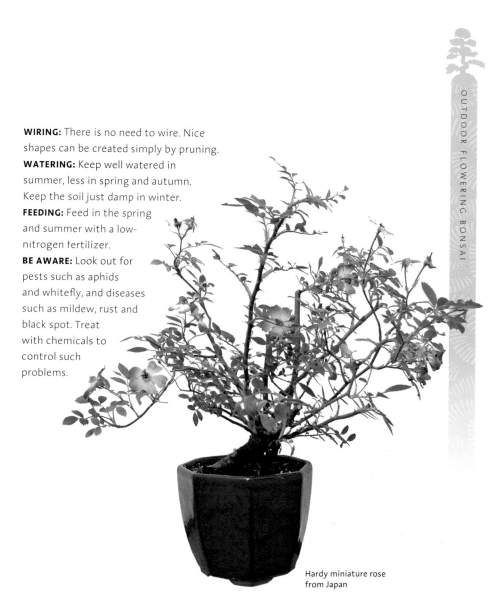

WIRING: There is no need to wire. Nice shapes can be created simply by pruning.

WATERING: Keep well watered in summer, less in spring and autumn. Keep the soil just damp in winter.

FEEDING: Feed in the spring and summer with a low-nitrogen fertilizer.

BE AWARE: Look out for pests such as aphids and whitefly, and diseases such as mildew, rust and black spot. Treat with chemicals to control such problems.

Hardy miniature rose from Japan

Rosmarinus officinalis

Rosemary

- *slightly tender*
- *very attractive as bonsai*
- *old specimens have interesting trunks*
- *scented foliage*

Rosemary is a native of southern Europe and the Mediterranean. It is long-lived in mild climates and can develop attractive, characterful trunks with age. Rosemary has highly scented, grey-green foliage and blue-white flowers, and these have traditionally been used for many culinary and medicinal purposes. It is not commercially available as bonsai, and good specimens are invariably made from plants collected from the wild, including from mountains (*yamadori*). Young plants from nurseries or from the garden can make attractive bonsai, but they need a substantial trunk to be convincing. Rosemary is a good plant to experiment with.

Above: Young stems of rosemary such as this one will turn woody as they mature. They need to be protected from frosts in winter.

Where to keep them

Rosemary (zones 4–7) is not winter hardy outside the Mediterranean region, and as bonsai they need winter protection. Keep in full sun in summer and protect from frost in winter in a conservatory or greenhouse.

How to look after them

REPOTTING: Repot every 3–4 years in spring. Use any free-draining compost.
PRUNING AND PINCHING: Prune and pinch regularly during the growing season.

WIRING: The soft shoots do not need wiring. Older shoots can be wired, but take care as they can be brittle.

WATERING: Rosemary does not need a lot of water. Allow the soil to dry out between waterings.

FEEDING: Feed regularly with a general fertilizer from spring to late summer to keep foliage healthy.

BE AWARE: Watch out for scale and other insect pests. Treat with an appropriate insecticide, as necessary.

Rosmarinus officinalis

Stewartia

Stewartia, stuartia

- hardy
- use deciduous plants for bonsai
- easy to keep
- white/creamy flowers
- attractive bark

Stewartias are closely related to *Camellia* (see pages 176–7), and there are some evergreen species in the genus. However, the species used for bonsai, *S. monadelpha* and *S. pseudocamellia* (Japanese stewartia, natsu-tsubaki), are both deciduous. They have pointed, oval leaves and mottled, cinnamon-coloured bark. The cup-shaped flowers are white. These plants are usually grown in the informal style. They are popular subjects for bonsai, and good examples can usually be found in bonsai nurseries.

Above: Stewartia flowers in mid-summer. The loose petals and prominent stamens resemble those of single-flowered camellias.

Where to keep them

Stewartia monadelpha (zone 6) is native to Korea and southern Japan and is hardy in temperate areas, while Japanese stewartia (zone 5) is also hardy. However, both species should be protected in a frost-free greenhouse or shed during prolonged periods of freezing weather in winter and early spring. In summer they can be kept in full sun, but when the flowers appear they should be shaded, to prevent the blooms being scorched.

How to look after them

REPOTTING: Repot stewartias every 2–3 years, in early spring. Use lime-free soil consisting of one part loam, one part Kanuma (or sphagnum moss peat) and one part sharp sand. Stewartias will not thrive in alkaline compost.

PRUNING AND PINCHING: Prune stewartias immediately after they have flowered, but be careful not to prune the shoots that develop during the growing season, because these carry next year's flowers. Lightly prune or pinch out the tips of the growing shoots at the end of the summer to maintain the overall shape of the tree. If the branches become too congested, some of the inner twigs can be removed, to allow air and light to penetrate and create a better structure.

WIRING: Do this in mid-summer. Leave the wires on for no longer than a year.

WATERING: Water regularly throughout the growing season, increasing the amount of water in summer. In winter, keep the compost just moist.

FEEDING: Immediately after flowering, apply a high-nitrogen fertilizer. This should be supplemented in late summer by a low-nitrogen fertilizer.

BE AWARE: Vine weevils can be a serious problem for stewartias. Check for the larvae when you are repotting. If you find any, remove and kill them, and then water nematodes into the compost in late spring. Aphids sometimes cluster on new shoots but can usually be removed by hand. A systemic insecticide can be applied if the problem persists.

Stewartia monadelpha

Styrax japonicus

Japanese snowbell

- *hardy*
- *deciduous*
- *easy to train*
- *bell-shaped flowers*
- *unusual fruit*

This beautiful flowering tree makes a fine bonsai. It has glossy, dark green leaves, which turn yellow or red in autumn. Dainty, bell-shaped, pinkish-white flowers, borne in early summer, are followed by tiny, aubergine-shaped fruits. Japanese snowbell is easy to train as bonsai and is suitable for most styles. Although it is seen only occasionally in general plant nurseries, it is usually available from good bonsai specialists.

Where to keep them

Japanese snowbell (zones 5–7) is a hardy species, which is native to China, Korea and Japan. It requires no special protection in the winter months and can be kept in full sun throughout the growing season.

How to look after them

REPOTTING: Repot young plants every other year, and older plants every 3–4 years. The best time to do this is early spring. Japanese snowbell does best in well-drained, fertile, loamy soil – Akadama soil with some additional organic material is ideal. It prefers neutral to acidic conditions.

Above: The dainty and delicate Japanese snowbell flowers are soon followed by tiny, aubergine-shaped fruits, which last well into autumn.

PRUNING AND PINCHING: Trim Japanese snowbell lightly in mid-summer and prune to shape in spring. The flowers are borne on the current season's shoots, so there is no danger of losing flowers from spring pruning. To keep the tree looking neat, pinch out growing tips of new shoots when two or three leaves have emerged, but take care not to remove the flower buds.

WIRING: Wiring is best done in winter or early spring. The wire should be left on for no more than a year.

WATERING: Water regularly during the growing season, especially in summer. If the compost dries out completely, the leaves will shrivel. Keep the compost just moist in winter.

FEEDING: Just after flowering, apply a high-nitrogen fertilizer. This should be followed by a low-nitrogen fertilizer in late summer.

BE AWARE: Japanese snowbell is generally trouble free, and as long as you water regularly it should live for many years. Branches on older trees sometimes suffer from die-back. If this happens, cut back to healthy tissue, and the stem will reshoot the following year.

*Styrax
japonicus*

Viburnum

Viburnum

- *hardy shrubs*
- *easy and care-free to grow*
- *characterful trunks on old specimens*

This is a large genus of both deciduous and evergreen shrubs, which grow mainly in the temperate regions of the northern hemisphere. The leaves of some species resemble those of _Acer_ (see pages 108–17). Most viburnum bear interesting flowers, some of which are large, showy and fragrant.

Where to keep them

Viburnum (zones 3–9) are hardy and need no special protection in winter. They like full sun.

How to look after them

REPOTTING: Repot every 2–3 years, in early spring. The compost should be free draining but not too sandy or peaty. Viburnums seem to prefer loam-based compost, like many other flowering plants.

PRUNING AND PINCHING: Prune after flowering, but do not cut too hard in late summer or you will remove the flowering shoots.

WIRING: Viburnums can be wired at any time, although late summer or winter is preferable.

Above: Many viburnum species have coarsely toothed leaves, which can sometimes be mistaken for those of maple.

WATERING: Provide lots of water during summer, less in spring and autumn. Keep the soil just moist in winter.

FEEDING: Feed viburnum with a high-nitrogen fertilizer in spring and a high-potash fertilizer in late summer to encourage flowering.

BE AWARE: Viburnums are susceptible to aphids and scale insects during the growing season. Spray with insecticide to eradicate these pests, or just wash the insects off with a strong jet of water.

Viburnum lantana

Vitis vinifera

Grapevine

- *fruiting tree or climber*
- *hardy*
- *easy to make into bonsai from old vine stumps*
- *always eye-catching*

Grapevine is a native climber of the Mediterranean region and much of central Europe. It is now widely grown all over the world, wherever it is hot and sunny, although it does prefer the type of climate to be found in the Mediterranean. Old plants, which have been pruned back regularly over the years, make excellent bonsai. The leaves, fruit and flaky bark are attractive and create interesting bonsai. As grapevine is not usually available as bonsai from commercial nurseries, it is very much a hobbyist's plant. It is easy to propagate from cuttings, or to turn nursery plants into bonsai.

Where to keep them

Although grapevine (zones 6–9) is frost hardy, as bonsai it needs some protection from hard frost. The combination of hard frost and wet conditions can kill grapevine bonsai during winter. It likes full sun in summer but do not let the leaves burn if the sun gets too hot. Some shade is advisable from scorching sun.

How to look after them

REPOTTING: Repot every 2–3 years, in spring, using free-draining, loamy

Above: When old, grapevines often develop a lovely flaky bark on the trunk.

compost. Use a deep bonsai pot –
grapevine never grows well in a
shallow pot.

PRUNING AND PINCHING: In late
summer, prune back to two or
three buds of the current season's
growth to encourage fruiting the
following year. Pinch back young
tendrils in summer. Do not prune
hard in winter, as you will prune
off the fruiting shoots.

WIRING: Wire in mid-summer.
Shaping can be achieved
without wiring, although if you
have to wire this may improve
the shape.

WATERING: Grapevine likes a lot of
water to swell its fruit and to keep
leaves turgid. Allow the soil to dry out
between waterings.

FEEDING: Feed once, with a low-nitrogen
fertilizer, after fruit have set. Feeding
before that will cause fruit to drop.

BE AWARE: Grapevine is prone to pests,
such as aphids and scale insects, and
diseases, such as mildew. Control them
with proprietary chemicals.

Vitis vinifera

Wisteria

Wisteria

- *hardy*
- *deciduous*
- *more challenging*
- *scented racemes in a range of colours*

Wisterias are the most beautiful of climbing plants, and the long, scented racemes of blue, purple, pink or white flowers look quite stunning. *Wisteria floribunda* (Japanese wisteria, fuji) and *W. sinensis* (Chinese wisteria) can both be trained as bonsai. Keeping the plants alive is not difficult, but getting them to flower year after year can be a challenge. Wisteria bonsai are still produced in large numbers in Japan for both the home and export markets. They are widely available in bonsai nurseries, and large specimens are much sought after by enthusiasts.

Most wisterias are deliciously scented, but Chinese wisteria is the most fragrant of all. The scent of white varieties is particularly strong.

Where to keep them

Wisterias (zone 6) are hardy plants and do not require special protection in winter. They do best if kept in full sun throughout the growing season.

How to look after them

REPOTTING: Repot every other year, in early spring or immediately after flowering, into free-draining, loam-based compost. Akadama soil mixed with a little sharp sand is ideal.

Left: *Wisteria floribunda* 'Violacea Plena' is a rare form of Japanese wisteria with double, mauve flowers.

PRUNING AND PINCHING: Prune back long tendrils to three buds in late summer. Branches that are too long should also be cut back at the same time. Do not prune in early spring or after late summer, because this will remove the potential flower buds. The growing tips of new wisteria shoots are not pinched out, as this will simply encourage the growth of lots of weak secondary shoots, which do not set flower buds.

WIRING: Pruning is sufficient to train wisterias. They do not require wiring.

WATERING: Wisterias need a lot of water throughout the growing season, especially when they are flowering, and in mid-summer. Some growers suggest standing the plant in a bowl of water at the height of summer, but leaving plants with their roots permanently in water for months on end will lead to root rot and possibly the death of the plant. It is better to stand the plant in a shallow bowl of water for no more than 3–4 hours on very hot days or simply water heavily several times a day in warm, dry weather. This should prevent the leaves from wilting. In winter, keep the compost just moist.

FEEDING: Apply a high-nitrogen fertilizer immediately after flowering. Feed again in late summer with a low-nitrogen one. Japanese rapeseed fertilizer is particularly beneficial for wisterias. A large handful in each pot after flowering should be enough to ensure repeat flowering.

BE AWARE: Scale insects can be a problem unless treated with a systemic insecticide.

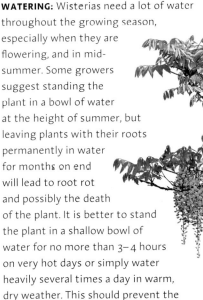

Wisteria floribunda 'Kuchi-beni'

Indoor/ tropical and subtropical BONSAI

Introduction

Indoor bonsai are a fairly recent development, introduced in the mid-20th century to meet the demand for bonsai that could be grown successfully inside the home. Like houseplants, indoor bonsai tend to be tropical and subtropical species that will survive in homes in temperate regions. Some Mediterranean and a few temperate species can also be adapted to grow indoors.

Care of indoor bonsai

Although indoor bonsai are slightly more difficult to manage than outdoor specimens, mastering their care is within the reach of everyone. The secret lies in selecting species that are easy to keep and in using simple growing aids to provide the conditions in which bonsai can do well. Plants generally do not grow well indoors, because there is insufficient light, humidity and fresh air. If these requirements can be met by artificial means, the plants will thrive. For example, improving light levels, by placing a fluorescent lamp above the bonsai, will make a world of difference. Similarly, humidity and warmth can be enhanced by standing the bonsai in a drip tray containing gravel or pebbles and by controlling the room temperature to suit the species.

Left: Most varieties of *Ficus* make good indoor bonsai. This is Chinese banyan (*Ficus microcarpa*).

Above: Serissa's variegated leaves are as attractive as its flowers.

Above: Bougainvillea offers a multitude of bright flower colours.

Indoor species

There are a number of species that are used as houseplants that make ideal indoor bonsai.

By far the most common indoor bonsai sold in temperate countries, in particular Europe and North America, is *Ulmus parvifolia* (see pages 310–11). This is also one of the easiest and most reliable plants for beginners. *Carmona microphylla* (see pages 254–5) and *Serissa foetida* (see pages 304–5) are also widely available, but they can be difficult for newcomers to bonsai, and do not make ideal 'starter' plants. Unless you can provide additional lighting and humidity, they will struggle in the average home. Many species of *Ficus*

(see pages 270–3), which are often grown as houseplants, make excellent and easy-to-grow indoor bonsai.

If you enjoy experimenting with plants, try growing other tropical and subtropical species and see how you get on. The range is enormous, and the following are just a few of those that have been used successfully by enthusiasts in various parts of the world and that are worth trying: *Bambusa ventricosa* (Buddha's belly bamboo), *Beaucarnea*, *Cassia*, *Cycas* (sago palm), *Euphorbia pulcherrima* (poinsettia), *Fortunella*, *Hibiscus*, *Ixora*, *Jacaranda*, *Lantana*, *Myrtus* (myrtle), *Nandina domestica* (heavenly bamboo) and *Nolina*.

Acacia

Acacia, Wattle, Thorn tree

- *tender*
- *lovely foliage and flowers*
- *very difficult as indoor bonsai in temperate zones*

This is an extremely large and diverse genus of more than a thousand species of deciduous and evergreen shrubs and trees. Acacias grow mainly in the tropical and subtropical parts of Australia and Africa, although some are found in warm temperate regions of the world. Apart from their economic value for food, medicine and a host of many other uses, some acacia species are well suited for bonsai, as has been demonstrated by bonsai enthusiasts in Australia and South Africa.

African acacias

The species mostly used for bonsai, especially in South Africa, are *A. burkei* (black-monkey thorn; zones 9– 10), *A. galpinii* (monkey thorn; zones 9– 10) and *A. nigrescens* (knob thorn; zones 7– 11).They are very suitable for the flat-top or Pierneef style pioneered by South African bonsai artists.

Australian acacias

Acacia paradoxa (kangaroo thorn; zones 9– 11), *A. dealbata* (mimosa; zones 8– 11)

Left: This beautiful bonsai acacia from South Africa has been grown in a natural tree style.

and *A. podalyriifolia* (Queensland silver wattle; zones 8–11) are good ones for bonsai. They are excellent for the weeping willow style.

Where to keep them

All acacias love full sun, but on very hot summer days need some shade to prevent leaves from burning. Acacia leaves fold up in strong sunshine, to reduce transpiration.

How to look after them

REPOTTING: Repot in early spring every two to three years, when roots become pot bound. Use free-draining compost consisting of one part loam, one part sand and one part grit.

PRUNING AND PINCHING: Prune new growth throughout the growing season, and cut back old growth in spring.

WIRING: Many of these species do not need much wiring, as pruning is usually sufficient to create nice shapes. Do any wiring of your acacia during the growing season.

WATERING: Although they do not require a lot of water year-round, do not let the soil dry out completely, otherwise the leaves will shrivel.

FEEDING: Feed regularly throughout the growing season with a general fertilizer.

BE AWARE: Keep an eye out for aphids, scale insects and woolly aphids. Treat them by washing them off with a jet of water or using an insecticide.

Acacia howittii

Adansonia digitata

Baobab

- *tender succulent*
- *easy to grow and keep*
- *very easy to propagate from seed*
- *deciduous tree*

Baobab is a long-lived deciduous tree, with a bulbous, succulent trunk, which grows best in dry, hot tropical regions of Africa and Asia. Some baobabs in Africa are more than a thousand years old. There is one in India with a trunk circumference of nearly 120m (394ft). This species branches readily and makes interesting bonsai in a relatively short time.

Where to keep them

This tender tree (zones 8–11) does not tolerate temperatures below 10°C (50°F). It loves full sun and high temperatures, so protect in cold weather and keep away from draughts.

How to look after them

REPOTTING: Repot every 2–3 years, in spring, with gritty compost. Any compost for cacti and succulents is also suitable for baobab.

PRUNING AND PINCHING: Prune in spring and pinch back new growth in summer to encourage branching.

Left: The leaves of baobab resemble those of figs. The trunk is similar to that of crassula.

WIRING: Baobab can be wired, but nice shapes can be created simply by pruning.

WATERING: Water less than you would other plants, as baobab is a succulent. In the winter, keep compost just damp.

FEEDING: Feed with a general fertilizer in the growing season. Excessive nitrogen will result in long, lanky shoots.

BE AWARE: Baobab is prone to aphids; treat by washing off with a jet of water or using an insecticide.

Adansonia digitata

Adenium

Desert rose

- *unusual shape*
- *showy flowers*
- *easy to grow in warm climates but difficult in cool-temperate ones*
- *popular flowering succulent*

These attractive perennial succulents originate from Africa and the Arabian peninsula. They are extremely popular as a bonsai in south and south-east Asia, where they are prized for their unusual bulbous shape and their attractive flowers. These range from deep red to pure white, and they appear during winter and spring in their native habitat. There is one very variable species, *Adenium obesum*.

Above: Desert rose flowers are available in a wide range of colours, from deep crimson to pure white. This is a bicoloured variety.

Where to keep them?

Desert roses (zones 10–11) cannot stand temperatures lower than 10°C (50°F). They need a warm, sunny location in order to flower well.

How to look after them

REPOTTING: Repot every couple of years, at any time of year. In fact, they flower better if kept pot bound.

PRUNING AND PINCHING: Shaping is normally achieved by pruning the new shoots after flowering.

WIRING: These succulents do not require wiring, although they can be wired.

WATERING: Being succulent, they do not like their roots wet. Keep them fairly dry. Water sparingly especially in winter, when once a week is plenty; water daily in summer, less in spring and autumn.

FEEDING: Use a general fertilizer in spring and a low-nitrogen one in late summer.

BE AWARE: Overwatering can cause the trunk to rot. Desert roses are also prone to fluffy scale; remove them by hand. Like most succulents, desert roses propagate easily from cuttings. They also grow easily from seed. Many interesting hybrids can be produced by cross-pollinating different plants.

Below: This desert rose is on display at the San Diego bonsai museum, where some fine examples of Californian species are grown.

Bougainvillea

Bougainvillea

- *tender*
- *evergreen*
- *challenging*
- *range of colours*
- *good for driftwood*

Most of the bougainvilleas available today are cultivars of *Bougainvillea glabra*, *B. spectabilis* and *B.* x *buttiana*, and they have been developed to provide a wide range of colourful bracts in shades of red, pink, mauve, yellow, orange and white. The bracts (often mistaken for flowers) are borne on the current year's growth of the thorny stems of these evergreen climbers. They are popular outdoor bonsai in southern and south-east Asia, but must be kept indoors in cool temperate regions. Bougainvillea are best grown in the informal upright style, and are very suitable for carving to create a hollow-trunk driftwood effect (see page 33).

Where to keep them

Bougainvilleas thrive in hot, sunny, dry conditions and are found mainly in tropical, subtropical and Mediterranean regions. *Bougainvillea glabra, B. buttiana and B. spectabilis* originate in Brazil, and even though *B. buttiana* is slightly less tender, none of these plants will survive a winter outdoors in temperate areas (zones 10–11). The long flowering season occurs mainly in the cooler winter months, but bougainvillea will not bloom well if kept outdoors in areas with excessive rainfall. Ideally, the winter temperature should be

8–15°C (46–59°F). When bougainvilleas are grown as indoor bonsai they must be kept in a warm, sunny room or a heated conservatory. If you do not have

Above: The yellow form of bougainvillea is rare, but it is no more difficult to care for than the common, mauve variety.

such conditions, you should provide supplementary heating and lighting.

How to look after them

REPOTTING: Repot every 3–4 years, during late spring. Use a loam-based, free-draining compost.

PRUNING AND PINCHING: Immediately after flowering, prune back hard to the old wood, to encourage new shoots to grow. The colourful bracts are carried on the current season's wood. Do not keep on pruning or pinching out the new growth, or you will have no bracts for the next year. If you want to carve the thick trunks to resemble the hollow trunks found in nature, do so in spring and summer, when cuts heal quickly.

WIRING: The shaping of bougainvilleas is achieved mainly through pruning, so wiring should not be necessary.

WATERING: During winter, allow the surface of the compost to dry slightly before you water. In spring, when the buds begin to develop, increase the amount of water so that the compost remains just moist, but never saturated. Misting is advisable if the room's atmosphere is very dry.

FEEDING: Apply a low-nitrogen fertilizer during the growing season.

BE AWARE: Bougainvilleas are prone to aphids, scale insects and red spider mites. Aphids can sometimes be picked off by hand, and misting will help control red spider mites. Treat severe infestations with systemic insecticides.

Bougainvillea

Calliandra

Powder-puff tree

- *tender tree*
- *beautiful foliage and flowers*
- *fast grower*
- *easy to make into bonsai*
- *trouble free*

This is a large genus of tropical and subtropical leguminous trees. The showy flowers look like a powder puff – hence its popular name. They range from deep crimson to white. *Calliandra haematocephala* has deep crimson flowers. Some species have thorny branches. Leaves are pinnate and soft – almost feathery. Powder-puff trees make stunning bonsai and are suitable for most styles. Beautiful examples can be seen in Florida, Brazil and Indonesia. Most hobbyists grow their powder-puff tree bonsai from seed or use nursery stock.

Where to keep them

Powder-puff trees (zones 9–11) are easy to grow in warm climates but not so suitable for cold temperate ones, even when grown as indoor bonsai. They prefer a warm, sunny position, although some enthusiasts have cultivated them successfully in shade.

How to look after them

REPOTTING: Repot frequently – perhaps every year, in spring or summer or in the

Left: The flowers of the powder-puff tree look like powder puffs – hence the common name.

rainy season in the tropics. Use compost consisting of equal parts loam and peat (or garden compost).

PRUNING AND PINCHING: Prune during the growing season, preferably after flowering.

WIRING: Shoots and branches take to wiring well, but exercise some care, as the branches are slightly brittle.

WATERING: Keep plants moist, year-round, but never soaking wet.

FEEDING: These are hungry plants and frequent feeding with a general fertilizer, in spring and summer, will keep them healthy and promote flowering.

BE AWARE: Calliandra may be infested by aphids, mealybugs, red spider mites and whitefly. Treat with appropriate insecticides.

Below: These semi-trained specimens of powder-puff trees are just eight years old. They are under cultivation in Brazil.

Callistemon

Bottlebrush

- *tender evergreen*
- *lovely flowers*
- *attractive foliage and bark*
- *easy in warm climates, but difficult as indoor bonsai in temperate climates*

These small evergreen trees or shrubs are natives of Australia. Many species, such as *Callistemon citrinus* (crimson bottlebrush) and *C. viminalis* (weeping bottlebrush), make excellent bonsai. They grow best in Mediterranean or subtropical climates, where they provide spectacular bonsai with their rough bark, evergreen foliage and bright red flowers. Bottlebrushes are tolerant of sea breezes so can be grown near the coast.

Where to keep them

Bottlebrushes (zones 9–11) are relatively trouble-free trees when grown as outdoor bonsai in warm climates, but as indoor bonsai in temperate zones they struggle, even when kept in a warm, sunny environment and given lots of light. A minimum temperature of 10°C (50°F) is best for them.

How to look after them

REPOTTING: Repot every couple of years, in spring, as they are vigorous growers. Use free-draining soil.

Left: Bottlebrush produces distinctive bark and foliage as well as lovely red flowers.

PRUNING AND PINCHING: Prune heavily after flowering. The following year's flowering shoots are then produced in late summer.

WIRING: Young shoots and branches can be wired. Do this in late summer or during winter.

WATERING: Water copiously during spring and summer, especially when bottlebrushes are flowering. Reduce watering when flowers are finished. Keep slightly dry in winter.

FEEDING: Apply a general fertilizer in spring and summer.

BE AWARE: Red spider mites, mealybugs and scale insects may cause problems; treat with appropriate insecticides.

Callistemon citrinus

Carmona microphylla, syn. *C. retusa*,
Ehretia buxifolia, *E. microphylla*

Fukien tea

- *tender*
- *evergreen*
- *challenging*
- *scented flowers*

This shrub is now grown extensively throughout Asia. It has glossy, dark green leaves and delicate, slightly scented white flowers. The greyish bark is fissured. Fukien tree stands up to pruning well, which makes it particularly suitable for bonsai.

It can be trained into most styles, particularly informal upright. It is widely available in bonsai nurseries, but it is not an easy plant and should not be taken on by newcomers to the hobby.

Where to keep them

Fukien tea (zone 10) is native to China, Japan, Korea and Taiwan, but is not hardy in temperate areas. Plants need warm, humid, bright conditions to do well; if you cannot provide these conditions they will struggle to survive. A windowsill in a warm, bright kitchen or lounge may be suitable, but ensure that the temperature never falls below 10°C (50°F) and that there are no sudden and wide temperature swings. Do not place Fukien tea in a draught. It will benefit from standing outside on warm, sunny days in summer.

How to look after them

REPOTTING: Repot every 2– 3 years, but only when the rootball is pot bound. Do

Left: Fukien tea has bright white flowers with a light scent, which appear at the ends of stems, like stars.

this in late spring. Use a fertile compost consisting of two parts leaf mould, one part loam and one part sharp sand.

PRUNING AND PINCHING: Prune sparingly and only to maintain the shape. Fukien tree flowers on the current season's wood, so take care that you do not remove new growth unless it is spoiling the shape of the tree. Prune in late winter or early spring, before the plant starts into growth. Pinch back the growing tips of secondary branches to two or three leaves, as soon as they have borne six or seven leaves. Continue to do this throughout the growing season.

WIRING: Although shaping of Fukien tea is mostly achieved through pruning, stems can be wired at any time of the year for no more than eight weeks.

WATERING: These plants like humid conditions, but water carefully so that the compost never becomes waterlogged. Keep the compost moist at all times, but in winter allow the surface to dry a little before watering. Plants will appreciate regular misting, to maintain a humid atmosphere.

FEEDING: It is best to apply a high-nitrogen fertilizer in the spring. In late summer, plants will benefit from a low-nitrogen one.

BE AWARE: This is a temperamental species and extremely difficult to grow as an indoor bonsai in temperate countries, although it does well in Mediterranean and subtropical climates. The leaves sometimes turn yellow and drop, which signifies too much water.

Carmona microphylla

Casuarina

Casuarina

- *evergreen tree*
- *makes lovely bonsai*
- *very easy subject for warm climates*
- *difficult as indoor bonsai in temperate zones*

This genus of evergreen shrubs and trees, which is native to Australia, the Pacific islands and south-east Asia, has spread to most tropical regions of the world. *Casuarina equisetifolia* (horsetail tree) is the species used for bonsai and, when well trained, resembles *Pinus thunbergii* (see pages 88– 9) in appearance. Despite its long, wispy needles, Indonesian bonsai artists have created some splendid masterpieces with this species.

Where to keep them

These tropical or subtropical plants (zones 9– 11) can be grown as an indoor bonsai in temperate climates but really do well only in the warm tropics. They can tolerate a temperature range of 10– 40°C (50– 104°F). Keep in full sun.

How to look after them

REPOTTING: Repot every other year, in spring or in the rainy season. Although casuarinas grow in any type of soil, they prefer sandy, volcanic, slightly acidic soil.

Left: A well-trained casuarina can easily be mistaken for a pine, whose foliage it strongly resembles.

After repotting, keep in a shady spot until new leaves emerge.

PRUNING AND PINCHING: Can be pruned at any time of year.

WIRING: Casuarinas take to wiring well, and this can be done at any time of year.

WATERING: They can withstand drought well, but water when the soil becomes dry. Do not overwater. Mist the foliage.

FEEDING: Use a general fertilizer in the growing season. Feed lightly, because casuarinas are naturally vigorous.

BE AWARE: Generally trouble free, but treat any problems as you would on other bonsai.

Casuarina equisetifolia

Celtis sinensis

Chinese hackberry, Japanese hackberry

- *hardy*
- *deciduous*
- *easy to keep*
- *orange fruits*

There are about 70 species in this genus, which belongs to the same family as *Ulmus* (see pages 164–7). Some are hardy and grow in northern temperate regions, while others are found in tropical Asia. They have an upright habit of growth and attractive bark, and they bear small, glossy, dark green leaves, small green flowers in spring and small orange fruits that ripen to reddish-brown. These plants are especially suitable for informal and formal upright bonsai styles. Chinese hackberry is very popular in China, from where large numbers of plants are exported for use as indoor bonsai.

Where to keep them

Chinese hackberry (zones 6–9), which is native to eastern China, Korea and

Japan, is fully hardy in temperate areas and can be kept outdoors where winter temperatures do not fall below -5°C (23°F). However, the plants imported as bonsai from China should be treated as indoor plants. They need maximum light to grow well and will do best on a bright, sunny windowsill. They should be turned regularly so that they do not 'lean' towards the light source. In winter,

Left: The glossy leaves of Chinese hackberry look fresh throughout summer. In autumn, they turn yellow and fall.

when the tree has shed its leaves, keep Chinese hackberry in a cool room, ideally no warmer than 8°C (46°F), so that it is temporarily dormant. Trees that are kept in conditions that encourage them to grow all year round quickly exhaust themselves and eventually die. In summer, Chinese hackberry benefits from standing outside in a sunny site.

How to look after them

REPOTTING: Repot every 2–3 years, in early spring. Use fertile, free-draining compost consisting of two parts loam and one part sharp sand.

PRUNING AND PINCHING: Prune between spring and the end of summer. Cut back overlong branches, and shorten new shoots that have three or four buds, pinching back to one or two buds.

WIRING: You can apply wires from spring to autumn if necessary, although most shaping is achieved by pruning.

WATERING: Water regularly and generously during the growing season, as soon as the surface of the compost feels dry. In winter, keep the compost just moist. This species will not survive in waterlogged soil. Misting is advisable if the room's atmosphere is very dry.

FEEDING: During the growing season apply a weak solution of a general liquid fertilizer every two weeks.

BE AWARE: Chinese hackberry is prone to aphids and red spider mites. Aphids can sometimes be picked off by hand, and misting will help control red spider mites. If the problem persists, apply a systemic insecticide.

Celtis sinensis

Citrus

Orange, Lemon

- *tender*
- *evergreen*
- *fragrant, white flowers*
- *yellow or orange fruits*

These plants make attractive, easy-to-keep bonsai. The mid- to pale green leaves are oval and borne on often spiny stems. The scented white flowers appear from late spring to summer and are followed by yellow or orange fruits. Also included in this group is *Fortunella hindsii* (dwarf kumquat), which is similar to *Citrus* but bears golden-yellow fruits. Plants are usually grown in the informal upright and broom styles. They are very common in Asia – especially around the lunar New Year in China, when fruits symbolize wealth – but are harder to get hold of elsewhere.

Where to keep them

All these plants are native to Mediterranean or subtropical areas, and they are tender in temperate areas (zone 10). They should be kept indoors, in good light, when temperatures fall below 3–5°C (37–41°F). In summer, place them outside in a sunny, sheltered position.

How to look after them

REPOTTING: Repot in late winter or early spring only when the roots are pot bound, which may not be more often than every three years. Use moisture-retentive, free-draining, neutral to acidic compost.

Above: Citrus bonsai are grown for their fragrant blossom and beautiful fruit. The fruits remain on the tree for a long time.

PRUNING AND PINCHING: Light pruning only is required for established indoor citrus bonsai. Trimming with scissors or pinching out of the growing tips will maintain the shape of the bonsai and encourage a fine framework. Pruning and pinching can be done in spring and summer, but be careful not to remove the flowering buds in the process. Thin out the twigs if the structure becomes too dense. Remove any fruits from the plant at the end of winter.

WIRING: Wire only when creating the bonsai structure. Do this in late spring, leaving the wires on for a year.

WATERING: Water freely in summer, making sure that the compost never dries out; water less in spring and autumn. At the same time, the rootball must never be waterlogged. These plants prefer to be kept drier in winter, in just moist compost. Misting is advisable if the room's atmosphere is very dry.

FEEDING: Feed these plants in summer after flowering and again when the fruits have set. Use a weak dose of a general fertilizer. If you give plants too much food, the leaves will turn yellow and drop.

BE AWARE: Overwatering and overfeeding can lead to leaf drop. Scale insects can be a problem and should be treated with a systemic insecticide.

Fortunella hindsii

Crassula

Crassula

- *tender*
- *succulent*
- *easy to keep*
- *attractive shape*

Two species – *Crassula arborescens* (silver jade plant) and *C. ovata* (syn. *C. portulacea*; jade plant, dollar plant) – from this large genus of succulent plants are particularly suitable for bonsai. They develop a tree-like habit with sturdy trunks and recognizable branches. Jade plant has the added advantage of small leaves, and a trunk and branches that can be wired into any shape. This species is used extensively for bonsai in India and South Africa, because it can be made into bonsai of all styles and sizes from *mame* bonsai to very large specimens.

Above: The small-leaved crassulas, such as this jade plant, make excellent tree-like bonsai, even though they are succulent plants.

Where to keep them

Both silver jade plant and jade plant (both zone 10) are native to southern Africa and should be regarded as tender plants. They can withstand minimum temperatures of 5– 7°C (41– 5°F). When grown as indoor bonsai, they should be kept in a bright position, although direct sunlight is not necessary for them to flourish.

How to look after them

REPOTTING: When grown in an indoor environment, repot every 4– 5 years, during late spring. Use free-draining compost, such as one of the proprietary cactus mixes, or one consisting of equal parts of loam, leaf mould and sharp sand.

PRUNING AND PINCHING: Maintain the shape of crassula bonsai during the growing season by trimming new shoots with scissors or pinching out the growing tips, pruning back to two or three pairs of leaves. This will encourage a fine branch framework. Hard pruning of indoor crassula is required only if you wish to change the structure of the tree.

WIRING: Jade plant has pliable branches that can be easily wired into any shape. The wires may be applied at any time of year, and they should be left on for about a year. Silver jade plant does not respond well to wiring, and so should be shaped by pruning alone.

WATERING: Crassulas prefer fairly dry conditions, so water sparingly in summer and give them even less in winter. Overwatering will cause the leaves of these species to grow large and floppy, making the tree top-heavy and unstable, or leading to root rot.

FEEDING: Feed once a month in summer, using a low-nitrogen fertilizer.

BE AWARE: Scale insects can be a problem and should be treated with a weak dose of systemic insecticide.

Aphids can usually be removed by hand, but if the infestation persists treat them with a systemic insecticide. Because crassulas are not repotted every year, vine weevils can be a problem. Water nematodes into the compost in late spring.

Crassula ovata

Cuphea hyssopifolia
False heather

- *bush rather than tree shape*
- *tender*
- *easy indoor subject in temperate climates*
- *protect from frost*
- *attractive flowers*

This is a tropical or subtropical evergreen shrub with small leaves and delicate white, mauve or crimson flowers. The scale of the leaves and flowers make it very suitable for bonsai. False heather will lose some leaves in winter, but this is normal for an evergreen. False heather is native to Central America, and is suitable for the broom or mophead style of bonsai.

Where to keep them?
False heather (zones 9–11) is a fairly easy plant to grow, provided it is kept at a minimum temperature of 10°C (50°F) Place in a bright sunny position if it is to flower well. Keep away from draughts.

How to look after them
REPOTTING: Repot every other year, in spring, using well-drained compost. A peat or coir-based compost is fine.
PRUNING AND PINCHING: False heather is usually just trimmed in a dome shape.

Right: False heather will flower continuously throughout the summer and into autumn. This is the mauve variety.

The branch structure is not that important.

WIRING: There is no need to wire.

WATERING: Water well in summer and less in winter. Just make sure that the plant does not dry out or get waterlogged.

FEEDING: Feed once a month in summer, using a general fertilizer.

BE AWARE: Prone to aphids and whitefly. Treat by washing off the bugs with a jet of water or by using a weak insecticide.

Cuphea hyssopifolia

Duranta erecta

Golden dewdrop

- *tender evergreen*
- *makes nice bonsai*
- *easy to keep and grow in warm climates*
- *can be grown as indoor bonsai in temperate countries*

Golden dewdrop is a vigorous, evergreen hedging shrub with golden-coloured foliage. It bears clusters of scented mauve flowers, which develop into orange berries. The flowers and berries are often borne on the plant at the same time. Most of the golden dewdrop bonsai come from Indonesia and China. Older specimens have thick characterful trunks and the wood is extremely hard. As an indoor bonsai, it is shy to flower or produce berries, unless you provide near-tropical conditions indoors.

Where to keep them

In the tropical and subtropical regions, golden dewdrop (zones 9–11) can be kept outdoors year-round in full sun. In temperate countries, it can be grown outdoors in summer to get maximum sunlight and fresh air, but should be kept indoors in winter, in a minimum temperature of 10°C (50°F). Indoor lighting would benefit this species when kept indoors.

How to look after them

REPOTTING: Repot every other year, in spring, as they are extremely vigorous. Use any well-drained soil.

PRUNING AND PINCHING: As they are a hedging plant, golden dewdrop tends to sucker from the base and from the trunk.

Right: Golden dewdrop leaves have this distinctive golden colouring, which is so attractive.

Duranta erecta

Prune off unwanted shoots and branches whenever they appear. Prune regularly and often to keep them looking tidy.

WIRING: As the stems are woody and hard, wiring can be difficult. Golden dewdrop responds well to wiring, although nice shapes can be created simply by pruning.

WATERING: Keep the soil moist year-round, and do not let the tree dry out.

FEEDING: Feed golden dewdrop regularly during the growing season, using a high-nitrogen fertilizer in spring and a low-nitrogen one later in the growing season.

BE AWARE: Control insect pests, such as red spider mites, whitefly and mealybugs when they appear; wash them off with water or apply an appropriate insecticide.

Eugenia

- *tender*
- *evergreen*
- *easy*
- *attractive foliage*
- *white flowers*
- *colourful fruit*

This is a large genus, belonging to the Myrtaceae family, of which two species – *Eugenia brasiliensis* (Brazilian cherry) and *E. uniflora* (Surinam cherry, pitanga) – are suitable for growing as bonsai. They have glossy, ovate leaves, which are tinged with bronze when they first emerge in spring. Clusters of fragrant white flowers are followed by colourful edible fruits, although plants can be difficult to get to fruit when they are grown as indoor bonsai. They are mainly grown in the informal upright style and are widely available from bonsai nurseries.

Where to keep them

Brazilian cherry and Surinam cherry (both zone 10) are native to Brazil. They should be kept in as bright a position as possible and somewhere that is warm and free from draughts. A sunny windowsill is suitable, but make sure that the temperature does not drop at night. Although both species are evergreen, they will lose their leaves if it gets too cold. You should aim to

Left: Eugenias have glossy green leaves and bark that flakes as the trees mature, adding interest to the trunks.

provide a minimum temperature of
15–18°C (59–65°F) with little fluctuation.

How to look after them

REPOTTING: Repot eugenias every
2–3 years. The best time of year to do
this is in spring, before the new leaves
emerge. A proprietary bonsai mix, such
as Kanuma, is suitable. Alternatively,
use a fertile, free-draining, loam-based
compost on the acidic side of neutral.

PRUNING AND PINCHING: Light pruning
only is required for eugenias grown
indoors in order to maintain the shape
of your bonsai. Prune and pinch out the
tips of new shoots during the growing
season, trimming back to two or three
new leaves.

WIRING: Although most shaping is
achieved through pruning, branches can
be wired. This should be done during
mid-summer, when the stems have
hardened. The wires can be left on for
about a year.

WATERING: Do not overwater. Water
sparingly in winter. Increase the amount
of water you give in spring and summer
but allow the surface of the compost to
dry between waterings.

FEEDING: A general fertilizer should
be applied once a month, from spring
until autumn.

BE AWARE: Eugenias grown as bonsai
rarely produce the colourful fruits for
which the species are grown in gardens.
Apart from needing a constantly warm
environment, these species are relatively
trouble free.

*Eugenia
uniflora*

Ficus

Fig

- *tender*
- *evergreen*
- *easy to keep*
- *very diverse*

This large genus of mostly evergreen shrubs and trees is found in tropical and subtropical areas throughout world. Many of the species have distinctive aerial roots, which grow from the trunk and branches. They make excellent houseplants and are therefore also good as indoor bonsai in temperate countries. They are among the most popular genera for bonsai, and large numbers are produced in China for export, and are available through the internet and in shops and bonsai centres.

The species are incredibly diverse, but the most popular ones for bonsai are *Ficus benjamina* (weeping fig), *F. microcarpa* (syn. *F. retusa*; Indian laurel; Chinese banyan) and *F. neriifolia*. Other species are summarized on pages 272–3.

Where to keep them

Weeping fig, Indian laurel and *F. neriifolia* are tender plants (zones 10–11) and will grow best at temperatures of 20–28°C (68–82°F), although they tolerate temperatures of 13–15°C (55–9°F) for short periods. They prefer a bright position in direct sunlight, but will also grow reasonably well in shade, especially weeping fig and Indian laurel. Keep them out of draughts. In summer, they can stand outside in a sunny position.

Left: Indian laurel has lovely, small leaves. It is also a very compact plant, which is why it is one of the most popular figs for indoor bonsai.

How to look after them

REPOTTING: Repot every 2–3 years. Although this can be at any time of the year, it is best done during spring. Use compost consisting of equal parts peat (or garden compost), sharp sand and loam.

PRUNING AND PINCHING: Hard pruning is not usually required in indoor environments. Keep the tree in shape during the growing season by trimming new shoots or pinching out the growing tips, pruning back to two or three leaves. Figs may also benefit from leaf pruning (partial or total defoliation; see page 30), in early summer. All figs exude a white milky sap when cut, but there is no need to apply paste to the wounds, because the sap will stop naturally.

WIRING: You can wire these plants at any time of the year. Remove the wires as soon as the branch has set, which may be only a few months.

WATERING: Keep the compost damp, but never waterlogged, by watering regularly but sparingly, although you can increase the amount of water slightly in summer. Most species of *Ficus* appreciate having their foliage misted from time to time, which also encourages aerial roots to form.

FEEDING: Apply a general fertilizer every 2–3 weeks during the growing season; reduce this to once a month in winter.

BE AWARE: All figs are susceptible to leaf loss if conditions change and to scale insects. To remove the insects, apply a weak dose of a systemic insecticide.

Ficus microcarpa 'Green Island'

Ficus

More fig species and cultivars

INDOOR/TROPICAL AND SUBTROPICAL BONSAI

- *tender*
- *evergreen/deciduous*
- *more challenging*
- *interesting*

An extensive range of varieties and cultivars derive from the more than 500 species of *Ficus*. They all have slightly different habits and leaf shapes. Specialist fig growers and bonsai enthusiasts in China, Taiwan, Indonesia, the Philippines, Hawaii and India have used them for many years. Unfortunately, many of them may not be readily available in Europe and North America, but it is only a matter of time before they find their way into these continents.

F. AUREA (FLORIDA FIG, STRANGLER FIG): The prolific aerial roots can strangle the host tree. It is best for large-sized bonsai on account of its large leaves, which are deep green.

F. BENGHALENSIS (BANYAN): The very large, thick leaves of this challenging but popular species look out of scale for bonsai. It can survive on poor, stony soil.

F. BENJAMINA VAR. NUDA, F. NATALENSIS, F. PELKAN, F. TOMENTOSA, F. VIRENS: These species have similar growth habits and are used extensively for bonsai on the Indian subcontinent. The medium-sized leaves are shed during winter, while the new leaves are tinged with pink in spring.

Left: Most figs have impressive root buttresses like this one. In time they fuse together to form a matted plate.

F. BURT-DAVII 'NANA' (VELD FIG): This easy-to-grow cultivar is very popular for bonsai, especially for *shohin* and *mame* trees, as it bears truly minute leaves.

F. BUXIFOLIA (BOX-LEAVED FIG): With its small leaves and good branching qualitites, this species is an excellent small-sized fruiting bonsai.

F. INFECTORIA, F. SALICIFOLIA: Both have similar habits and longer leaves than most other figs.

F. MICROCARPA 'LONG ISLAND': Many subcultivars, with small leaves, short internodes, masses of aerial roots and interesting bark, have been bred from the original plants.

F. RELIGIOSA (BO TREE), F. RUMPHII: These very popular species in India and south-east Asia make excellent bonsai. They bear pointed, heart-shaped leaves; new leaves are pink/bronze.

F. RUBIGNOSA (PORT JACKSON FIG): This easy variety is widely used for bonsai in southern hemisphere countries. It has medium-sized to large leaves.

Where to keep them

These figs (zones 8–11) prefer warm, bright conditions – 19–30°C (66–86°F). They can be placed near a radiator in winter, provided the soil is not allowed to dry out. They also grow better under artificial lighting. Keep them out of draughts. In summer they can stand outside in a sunny position.

How to look after them

Treat these plants in same way as the figs listed on pages 270–1.

Ficus rumphii

Fuchsia

Fuchsia

- *tender or half-hardy*
- *deciduous/evergreen*
- *easy to keep*
- *range of colours*

The hundred or so species in this genus have been hybridized to produce more than 8,000 cultivars, and it is possible to find the colourful and distinctive flowers in every imaginable shade of pink, red, purple and orange as well as white. The tender and half-hardy plants make excellent indoor bonsai, especially those that have tiny leaves and flowers, and they are suitable for small and mini-bonsai. Fuchsias are not usually seen in bonsai nurseries, because this group of plants tends to be grown only by amateur enthusiasts.

Where to keep them

Fuchsias are native to mountainous areas of New Zealand and Central and South America. Although some species and cultivars are hardy, most are tender or, at best, half-hardy (zones 6–10). They will do best in a bright position, such as on a windowsill, especially during the growing season. When the plant is dormant in winter, light is not as important. Tender fuchsias require a warm environment (15–20°C/59–68°F). Hardy and half-hardy plants can be kept at 5–15°C (41–59°F). Fuchsias placed in temperatures above 4–5°C (40–41°F) all year round will remain evergreen.

How to look after them

REPOTTING: Repot each year, from early to late spring, or when pot bound. They also need fertile, moisture-retentive

Above: The dangling flowers of fuchsia are immediately recognizable. Cultivars with small leaves and tiny flowers are ideal for bonsai.

but free-draining compost containing plenty of organic matter. Use a mixture consisting of three parts peat (or garden compost), one part loam and one part sharp sand. If possible, add some leaf mould to the compost.

PRUNING AND PINCHING: As fuchsias flower on the current season's shoots, pruning should be done in early spring. After the first flowering, deadhead the flowers and trim the plant again. Most fuchsias will produce two crops of flowers in a year. If pinching out new shoots to maintain the shape, be sure not to remove too many flower buds.

WIRING: Fuchsias have soft stems and should not be wired.

WATERING: Make sure that fuchsias do not dry out. Water regularly throughout the growing season, and keep the compost just moist in winter. Mist them if the room's atmosphere is very dry.

FEEDING: During the growing season, apply a high-nitrogen liquid fertilizer every two weeks. When fuchsias are in flower, switch to a low-nitrogen one. These plants will also benefit from foliar feeds from time to time. Stop feeding fuchsias by late summer.

BE AWARE: Fuchsias are susceptible to aphid infestation from spring to late summer. Spray infested plants with a gentle insecticide. Mildew can also be a problem with plants that are not carefully watered. Remove and burn infected leaves and apply an appropriate fungicide.

Fuchsia reflexa

Gardenia jasminoides, syn. *G. augusta*

Common gardenia, Cape jasmine

- *tender*
- *evergreen*
- *easy to keep*
- *attractive foliage*
- *scented, white flowers*

Common gardenia has become a popular houseplant, because of its beautiful white, scented flowers and glossy, dark green leaves. It is not surprising that it is also now used for indoor bonsai. A number of different cultivars are grown, including some with small, variegated leaves. Common gardenia is fairly easy to keep but will not flower profusely unless grown in a heated greenhouse. The informal upright style is best for this species.

Above: The gardenias used for bonsai in Japan have small leaves and tiny flowers, which set orange fruit if pollinated.

Where to keep them

Common gardenia (zones 8–11), which originated in China, Taiwan and Japan, is a tropical plant and needs a minimum temperature of 10–15°C (50–59°F). It requires a bright position but should not stand in direct sunlight. Protect from draughts and cold. If you keep it on a windowsill, move it to a warmer spot at night and when the curtains are drawn. Stand outside in partial shade in summer.

How to look after them

REPOTTING: Repot common gardenia every two years, in early spring. It needs lime-free (ericaceous) compost, which must be fertile and free-draining. Use a mix consisting of two parts loam, one part leaf mould and one part sharp sand.

PRUNING AND PINCHING: Hard pruning is required only if the plant has lost its shape or become congested. Otherwise, prune after flowering to maintain a good overall shape. Avoid pruning in mid-summer, so you do not remove any of the flowering shoots. As soon as new secondary shoots bear six or seven leaves, pinch them back to three leaves.

WIRING: Gardenia bonsai does not usually require wiring. However, if you want to shape one of the stems, wait until it has become woody and hard. Leave the wires on for no longer than a year.

WATERING: Water common gardenia regularly and freely during the growing season, reducing the amount in autumn and keeping the compost moist in winter. Make sure that the rootball never dries out. The foliage will benefit from regular misting.

FEEDING: Apply a high-nitrogen fertilizer in spring, and a low-nitrogen one in summer. Common gardenia also appreciates a foliar feed in spring.

BE AWARE: Common gardenia must have a fairly constant temperature to thrive. It is susceptible to sap-sucking pests, such as scale insect, aphids and whitefly. Treat them with a systemic insecticide if there are too many to pick off by hand. Mildew can also be a problem when there is little movement of air around the leaves. Remove and burn infected leaves, apply fungicide if necessary and water carefully.

Gardenia jasminoides

Ilex crenata

Japanese holly, Box-leaved holly

- *hardy*
- *evergreen*
- *easy to keep*
- *glossy foliage*
- *black berries*

This hardy, evergreen holly has glossy, dark green leaves with scalloped (not spiny) edges. In summer, it produces small white flowers, and these are followed by black berries. When Japanese holly is grown indoors, it is reliable and easy to keep as long as it is placed in a fairly cool position. Large numbers of bonsai are produced in China for the indoor bonsai market elsewhere in the world. They are most suited to the informal upright and cascade styles.

Where to keep them

Although Japanese holly (zones 7–10) is a hardy plant, native to Russia, Japan and Korea, when grown as a bonsai it is regarded as an indoor subject. Keep it in a bright location, such as a windowsill, and in summer it will benefit from a spell outdoors. In winter, Japanese holly prefers a room that is cool rather than one that is too warm so that it can undergo a period of dormancy.

How to look after them

REPOTTING: Repot every other year, during late spring. Japanese holly needs

Above: The leaves of a healthy Japanese holly are shiny and oval, resembling the foliage of box.

a moisture-retentive but free-draining mix consisting of equal parts loam and leaf mould. You may need to add some sharp sand, to improve the drainage.

PRUNING AND PINCHING: In early spring, after the new shoots have hardened, prune back the new growth to maintain the shape of your bonsai. If you want berries to form, do not prune away the shoots that bear the flowers in summer. Pinch out the growing tips of new shoots, as necessary, to keep the tree looking trim.

WIRING: If necessary, wiring can be done in early spring. Protect the stems with raffia, because they can be brittle. Retain the wiring for two years, to allow the branches to set.

WATERING: Water regularly, increasing the amount when the flowers appear, to encourage the formation of berries. Allow the surface of the compost to dry slightly between waterings. Keep the compost just moist in winter, but never allow it to dry out completely. Misting is advisable if the room's atmosphere is very dry.

FEEDING: Apply a general fertilizer throughout the growing season.

BE AWARE: The young shoots of Japanese holly are sometimes infested with aphids, but these can usually be removed by hand or with a jet of water. Apply a systemic insecticide if the problem persists. Overwatering can sometimes lead to root rot.

Ilex crenata

Lagerstroemia indica
Crepe myrtle

- *difficult indoor variety for temperate climates*
- *requires very warm and bright conditions to do well*
- *beautiful flowers resemble crepe paper*
- *easy to bonsai*

Crepe myrtle is grown primarily for its showy flowers, which are borne in bunches on the tips of the branches. They come in pink, red, mauve and white. It is best to grow crepe myrtle as an outdoor bonsai in Mediterranean, tropical and subtropical areas, where it makes fine bonsai. As an indoor bonsai in temperate countries, it will struggle, but provided you give it warm and sunny conditions it can be persuaded to flower. Crepe myrtle is not a long-lived tree, because the wood is soft and termites love to eat it.

Where to keep them?

This tree (zones 7–11) is native to the tropical parts of India and China and will thrive only in warm, sunny conditions. If grown as an indoor bonsai in temperate climates, it needs a very bright and warm position to survive. A heated conservatory or greenhouse is the best environment for this plant, because temperatures should never fall below 15°C (59°F). Maintain an even temperature, especially in winter.

Left: Crepe myrtle produces bunches of lovely flowers in spring and early summer. It offers an attractive species for bonsai.

How to look after them

REPOTTING: Repot every other year, in early spring, but remove only the minimum amount of soil. Use compost consisting of equal parts loam and organic matter.

PRUNING AND PINCHING: Prune the branches immediately after flowering, or in autumn if you have not had any flowers that year. Shaping can be achieved by pruning.

WIRING: Wiring is not necessary.

WATERING: Water often when the tree is growing and producing new shoots, which is in spring. At other times, just keep the soil moist. Make sure the soil is never soaking wet.

FEEDING: Feed in spring before flowering, with a general fertilizer.

BE AWARE: A sudden drop in temperature can do a lot of harm. Even when grown in the tropics, crepe myrtle wood is prone to rotting. Watch out for mealybugs, red spider mites and whitefly; wash off or treat with appropriate insecticides.

Lagerstroemia indica

Ligustrum lucidum, Ligustrum sinense

Chinese privet

- *hardy*
- *evergreen/deciduous*
- *white flowers*
- *blue-black berries*

Ligustrum lucidum (Chinese privet) and *L. sinense* belong to the same genus as *L. vulgare* (see pages 144–5), which is grown as an outdoor bonsai. Chinese privet is an evergreen plant with small, glossy, dark green leaves, white flowers and blue-black berries, while *L. sinense* is a deciduous species, with light green leaves, white flowers and purple-black berries. Both these species are fast growing and easy to train as bonsai (usually in the informal upright style), and vast numbers are exported from China.

Where to keep them

Chinese privet (zones 7–11) is native to China, Korea and Japan, while *L. sinense* (zones 7–11) originated in China. Both are hardy plants that can be grown outdoors, where they do well. If grown as indoor subjects, they need a bright, sunny but not too warm position, and both species benefit from being moved outdoors in summer. If they are too warm indoors, especially in winter, they will produce leggy shoots. Variegated forms show better coloration when placed in full sun.

Left: The leaves of the privet used for indoor bonsai are slightly rounded and a lighter shade of green than the common privet grown for hedging.

How to look after them

REPOTTING: Repot every other year, from mid- to late spring. They prefer free-draining compost, such as one consisting of two parts loam and one part sharp sand, but they are not fussy plants and will grow in almost any compost as long as it is not waterlogged.

PRUNING AND PINCHING: These species require light pruning, in mid-summer, to maintain their shape. Pinch out the growing tips of new shoots, as necessary, to keep the bonsai trim.

WIRING: Wire branches in summer. Remove the wires if they are biting deeply into the bark. Initial training wires can be left on for 1–2 years, while the branches set.

WATERING: Water regularly but take care that you do not overwater. The compost should be kept moist all year round, but give more water in summer, when plants are growing. Misting is advisable if the room's atmosphere is very dry.

FEEDING: Feed with a general fertilizer once every 2–3 weeks during spring and summer.

BE AWARE: Chinese privet and *L. sinense* are susceptible to sap-sucking insects, such as scale insects, aphids and whitefly. Spray or apply a systemic insecticide if there are too many to pick off by hand. Branches sometimes die back for no apparent reason. If this happens, cut the affected stems back to healthy tissue.

Ligustrum sinense

Loropetalum chinense

Chinese fringe flower

- *tropical/subtropical*
- *attractive foliage and flowers*
- *easy as indoor bonsai in temperate countries*
- *tolerates some frost*

There are just a few species in the *Loropetalum* genus; some have green leaves and there is one (*L. chinense* var. *rubrum*) that has rich burgundy-coloured leaves. Flowers are deep pink and feathery in appearance – similar to those of *Hamamelis* (witch hazel) – both being members of the witch hazel family. Chinese fringe flower is a handsome plant, which is becoming more popular in many temperate countries as a semi-hardy bonsai. This native of China and Japan is a semi-evergreen shrub or small tree best suited to tropical and subtropical climates.

Above: The delicate petals of the Chinese fringe flower resemble a fringe or tassel – hence its common or popular name.

Where to keep them

Chinese fringe flower is suitable for zones 7– 11, but can tolerate some frost. In temperate climates, it can be grown outdoors in summer, but requires winter protection from hard frosts. Chinese fringe flower can be placed in sun or semi-shade in warm climates, but in temperate climates it prefers full sun.

How to look after them

REPOTTING: Repot once every 2– 3 years, in spring, using humus-rich, slightly acidic compost.

PRUNING AND PINCHING: Keep well pruned in summer to encourage bushiness.

WIRING: Chinese fringe flower does not need wiring, because the desired shape can be created simply by pruning.

WATERING: Although drought tolerant, it should be kept well watered during the growing season. Keep damp during the winter.

FEEDING: Feed with a high-nitrogen fertilizer in spring and early summer. In late summer, use a low-nitrogen feed.

BE AWARE: Chinese fringe flower is not prone to pest attack or diseases.

Loropetalum chinense

Murraya paniculata

Satin wood, Jasmine orange, Chinese box

- *tender*
- *evergreen*
- *challenging*
- *fragrant flowers*
- *bright red berries*

This attractive shrub or small tree has pinnate, glossy, dark green leaves and smooth grey bark. Strongly scented, white flowers are borne in clusters – all year round where it is warm enough – and are followed by round, red berries. Satin wood is a difficult species to grow successfully as an indoor bonsai and cannot be recommended as a 'starter' plant. It is suitable for any bonsai style except windswept. This plant is very common in Asia and other tropical regions, but harder to find elsewhere.

Where to keep them

Satin wood (zone 10) is native to tropical areas of south-east Asia, China and India. In addition to providing humidity and good light, it must be kept in a warm, draught-free place with a minimum temperature of 18°C (65°F).

How to look after them

REPOTTING: Repot satin wood bonsai every 2–3 years, in spring. It needs a fertile, free-draining mix of two parts loam, one part peat (or garden compost) and one part sharp sand.

Above: Satin wood leaves are a bright shiny green and highly aromatic. The wood of this tree is extremely dense and hard.

PRUNING AND PINCHING: Heavy pruning to shape the bonsai plant can be done in spring, as well as light pruning throughout the growing season. Be careful not to remove the flowering shoots. Cut or pinch back the shoots to two leaves, as soon as five or six new leaves have emerged.

WIRING: Satin wood is grown extensively throughout Asia for the hardness of its wood, and woody branches are almost impossible to bend with wire, so any shaping must be done before the stems harden. Young, semi-hard stems can be wired at any time, but do not leave the wire in place for more than eight weeks.

WATERING: This species needs moisture all year round. In summer, water before the compost begins to dry out and stand the pot on a tray of pebbles or gravel to increase humidity. In winter, keep the compost moist. Mist the foliage regularly.

FEEDING: Apply a general fertilizer every two weeks from spring to late summer. In autumn, apply a low-nitrogen feed.

BE AWARE: You will need to check regularly for aphids and greenhouse whitefly, which often leave sticky honeydew on the leaves, on which sooty mould develops. Aphids can be picked off by hand. You should also mist to clean the leaves and apply a systemic insecticide if any problem persists. Red spider mites may appear if satin wood is not kept in a sufficiently humid environment.

*Murraya
paniculata*

Pemphis acidula
Pemphis

- *tropical tree*
- *very popular in Indonesia*
- *stunning bonsai*
- *challenging*

Pemphis is a wild coastal plant that grows near mangrove swamps in the tropics around the Indian Ocean and South China Sea. It has been introduced to the bonsai world only fairly recently by Indonesian bonsai growers, who have made some exquisite specimens with this material. The wood is extremely hard and durable, which makes it ideal for driftwood effects (see page 33). This is very much a connoisseur's plant for bonsai hobbyists and collectors, and is not normally available as commercial bonsai.

Where to keep them

This vigorous and prolific grower (zones 9–11) can survive harsh growing conditions. However, it likes to be sprayed with sea water in order to flourish, which may pose a problem for those who do not live near the sea. Pemphis is very easy to grow as an outdoor bonsai in tropical or subtropical climates. It must be kept in full sun and in an open location. As it cannot tolerate cold temperatures – anything below 10°C (50°F) will damage or kill it – it can be difficult to grow as an indoor bonsai in temperate climates. It needs strong artifical light and warm, humid hothouse conditions.

Above: Although not grown for its flowers, pemphis blossom is very attractive too.

How to look after them

REPOTTING: Repot every other year, in spring, because it is an extremely vigorous plant. Pemphis needs well-drained, open compost. Indonesian and Philippine growers use volcanic grit or clinker as the growing medium, because this provides good drainage as well as having water-retention properties.

PRUNING AND PINCHING: Prune regularly, year-round, as it is a fast grower.

WIRING: Pemphis takes to wiring well. and should be done in early spring. The wires can be left on for 1–2 years.

WATERING: Keep well watered at all times, because pemphis is a coastal plant. Spray the plant occasionally with sea water.

FEEDING: Feed regularly especially during summer, less so in winter. Use any type of chemical or organic fertilizer.

BE AWARE: Watch out for caterpillars on the leaves. The roots are also prone to nematode problems. Treat with appropriate chemicals to combat these problems.

Pemphis acidula

Pistacia lentiscus

Lentisc, Mastic tree

- *evergreen*
- *half-hardy*
- *easy to keep*
- *good for indoors*
- *fast growing*

This vigorous Mediterranean shrub has been cultivated for thousands of years for its precious resin, which is edible and has been used for centuries as a mastic and as an aromatic gum or spice. It is also a medicinal plant. Lentisc is dioecious, there being male and female plants. All have attractive green foliage and red-tinged stems – the male plants produce red flowers while the females bear green ones. The use of lentisc for bonsai is only fairly recent. It makes a lovely plant as an outdoor bonsai in Mediterranean and subtropical regions. It can also be grown as an indoor bonsai in temperate climates.

Above: Lentisc foliage looks good and exudes a lovely aromatic fragrance.

Where to keep them

This tough plant (zones 8– 10) grows in poor, arid soil. It can tolerate salt-laden winds, which sweep off the sea, as well as some frost. In temperate areas, treat lentisc as an outdoor plant in the summer months but provide some winter protection from very hard frost. This plant loves full sun.

How to look after them

REPOTTING: Repot every other year, in spring, because it is a vigorous grower. Use free-draining, sandy soil.

PRUNING AND PINCHING: Prune regularly in summer right through to late autumn.

WIRING: Lentisc can be wired, although lovely shapes can be created just by pruning this vigorous shrub.

WATERING: Although lentisc is a Mediterranean plant which grows in arid regions, it still requires regular watering. Keep the compost moist at all times.

FEEDING: Feed your plant in the growing season, with a half-strength general fertilizer.

BE AWARE: Lentisc can be susceptible to scale insects. Treat with insecticide.

*Pistacia
lentiscus*

Pithecellobium tortum

Brazilian rain tree

- *best for tropics*
- *vigorous*
- *difficult as an indoor bonsai*
- *versatile for any style or design*

One of the legume family, Brazilian rain tree is a small, fast-growing tree with compound leaves, hard wood and thorny branches. It is a true tropical and loves a warm climate. Its characteristic, wide, undulating trunk and deep green bark mean it is a truly beautiful species for bonsai.

Where to keep them

Brazilian rain tree (zones 10–11) should really only be grown as bonsai in tropical and subtropical climates, where it is easy to look after. If used as an indoor bonsai in temperate climates, it needs a minimum temperature of 10°C (50°F), high humidity and high light levels. In the tropics, it likes a bright, sunny position for most of the year, although in summer it should be protected from strong, hot sun.

How to look after them

REPOTTING: Repot every other year, in spring, using free-draining compost. This can be sandy loam or just sand.

Left: Brazilian rain tree produces distinctive mid-green foliage and lovely bark. Its trunk is also very interesting and characterful.

PRUNING AND PINCHING: Prune regularly with scissors. Trim to an outward-pointing bud, so that shoots do not grow inwards.

WIRING: Branches can be wired, but be careful of the thorns when doing this. The main branches can be wired into position during initial styling, but once this is achieved there is no need to wire further. Remove the wire as soon as each branch has set, to prevent the bark disfiguring.

WATERING: Keep moist year-round, but not too wet as the roots can rot.

FEEDING: Feed Brazilian rain tree during the growing season, with a half-strength, organic or chemical fertilizer of any type.

BE AWARE: Brazilian rain tree attracts mealybugs, red spider mites and whitefly when grown indoors; treat with insecticide.

Pithecellobium tortum

Podocarpus

Podocarpus

- *half-hardy*
- *evergreen*
- *easy to keep*
- *interesting bark*
- *red-purple berries*

Two species of podocarpus are used for indoor bonsai: the short-leaved *P. nivalis* (Alpine totara) and the longer-leaved *P. macrophyllus* (Chinese yew, kusamaki, Buddhist pine). The latter develops into a conical tree with attractive, red-brown bark. The leaves are dark green, lighter beneath, and held in upright shoots, known as candles. Red-purple berries are borne on female plants in autumn. Chinese yew is suitable for most bonsai styles except windswept and is widely available from bonsai nurseries. Alpine totara is very similar in habit to Chinese yew, except that it can tolerate slightly lower winter temperatures.

Above: The leaves of podocarpus resemble yew. This is Alpine totara, the small-leaved variety.

Where to keep them

Chinese yew (zones 7– 11) is native to China and Japan, while Alpine totara (zones 6– 9) comes from New Zealand. They prefer cool conditions, in summer and winter. In temperate areas, keep them in a bright position or partial shade in winter, at a temperature of 6– 20°C (43– 68°F), and stand outside in summer in full sun.

How to look after them

REPOTTING: Repot every 2– 3 years, in late spring, taking care not to damage the roots, which are particularly sensitive. Use fertile, moisture-retentive but free-draining compost consisting of one part loam, two parts leaf mould and one part sharp sand.

PRUNING AND PINCHING: Prune the growing tips at any time while the plant is in growth. Unlike *Taxus* (see pages 98– 9), these plants will not regenerate from old wood, so take care of the bark when you cut. Use small, sharp clippers to cut out candles, which are too tough to pinch out with fingers. Do not cut through the needles, which will become discoloured and might lead to die-back.

WIRING: Wire at any time of year. Wait for young stems to harden before wiring them, and remove the wire after 8– 10 weeks.

WATERING: Keep the compost moist all year round, but do not overwater, as this will cause the leaves to turn grey, wither and drop. Mist the foliage in summer or use a watering can with a rose to 'shower' the plant, which cleans and freshens the foliage.

FEEDING: From spring until late summer, apply a high-nitrogen fertilizer once a month. In early autumn, give one application of a general fertilizer.

BE AWARE: Podocarpus leaves attract woolly aphids, but these can be picked off by hand or controlled with a systemic insecticide.

Podocarpus nivalis

Premna

Premna

- *coastal plant for tropical climates*
- *leaves attractive but smelly*
- *difficult as indoor bonsai in temperate countries*

Discovered only recently by Indonesian bonsai artists as good bonsai material, this vigorous plant is likely to become the bonsai superstar of the future. It can be used for any style. Premna is a tropical and subtropical plant that grows mainly in south-east Asia but is also found in southern China, Taiwan, Philippines and Australia. There are many species, but *Premna microphylla* and *P. serratifolia* are the favourites with bonsai enthusiasts on account of their dainty leaves, which have an obnoxious odour, similar to *Serissa foetida* (see pages 304– 5). The trunks have great character, with natural driftwood similar to that of 'Shimpaku' juniper (see pages 58– 9).

Above: Premna bonsai is grown mainly for its characterful trunk. The foliage is not distinctive.

Where to keep them

Premna (zones 8– 11) bonsai are easy to care for in tropical and subtropical regions, where they need a bright, sunny location. As indoor bonsai in temperate zones they require lots of light, high humidity and temperatures no lower than 10°C (50°F).

How to look after them

REPOTTING: Repot every other year, in spring or in the rainy season. Use well-drained, sandy soil.

PRUNING AND PINCHING: Prune to shape, using scissors or secateurs. Constant pruning will create an excellent framework.

WIRING: The trunks, branches and twigs have so much character that they do not require any wiring.

WATERING: Like most south-east Asian trees, they like lots of water in the growing season. Keep moist in winter.

FEEDING: Feed with a general fertilizer in the growing season.

BE AWARE: Attack from aphids and other sap-sucking insects are a real problem. Spray as soon as pests are detected. Insects sometimes penetrate the bark and cause branches to die back.

Premna microphylla

Punica granatum

Pomegranate

- *half-hardy*
- *deciduous*
- *orange flowers*
- *pretty fruits*
- *interesting trunks*

Although the genus contains two species, only *Punica granatum*, which produces the well-known fruit, is widely grown. It has narrow, glossy, bright green leaves, which are tinged with bronze or red when they first emerge. It also bears orange-red flowers and yellow-brown fruits. The dwarf form *P. granatum* var. *nana* is grown mainly for its beautiful, orange-pink flowers and tiny fruit. In Japan, cultivars with twisted, gnarled trunks are highly prized. Pomegranate is usually trained into the informal upright style and it is widely available from bonsai nurseries.

Where to keep them

Pomegranate (zone 7) is native to a wide area from south-east Europe to the Himalayas, and is half-hardy in temperate areas. It flowers only in full sun, and fruits will form in autumn only in temperatures of 13–16°C (55–61°F). In winter, when pomegranate has no leaves, the temperature can be as low as 3°C (37°F), and plants will even tolerate 0°C (32°F) for short periods. Plants that are too warm in winter develop weak, straggly shoots. Move indoor bonsai outdoors in summer, to a position in full sun; if this is not possible, keep it in a sunny spot indoors.

Above: The fruit of *Punica granatum* 'Nana' sets easily in summer and will remain on the plant until the following spring.

How to look after them

REPOTTING: Repot every 3–4 years, during early spring. Use fertile, free-draining compost consisting of two parts loam and one part sharp sand.

PRUNING AND PINCHING: Prune the new shoots after flowering if they have grown too long. Pinch out the growing tips to maintain the shape of the plant and stimulate the growth of new flowering shoots. Avoid pruning and pinching out these plants in summer, because this will remove the flowering buds from the shoot tips.

WIRING: Branches can be wired from the end of spring until summer. Leave the wires in place for about a year.

WATERING: Water the plants regularly in summer, making sure that the compost never dries out. In winter, keep the compost just moist. Mist the leaves in summer.

FEEDING: From early spring to summer apply a general fertilizer once a month. In late summer, use a low-nitrogen feed.

BE AWARE: Sap-sucking insects, such as scale insects, aphids and whitefly, can be a problem for this species. They can be picked off by hand or removed through the use of a systemic insecticide or by spraying as soon as they are noticed. The trunks of old plants rot easily, so never let moss grow around the base.

Punica granatum

Sageretia thea, syn. S. theezans

Sageretia, Bird plum cherry

- *tender*
- *semi-evergreen*
- *easy to keep*
- *attractive bark*
- *black berries*

This species is widely used for bonsai. It has an upright habit, small, glossy leaves and small, black berries. The greyish bark peels away in irregular patches to reveal lighter grey beneath. This is a great favourite with bonsai enthusiasts in China and is a popular indoor bonsai, which can be recommended for newcomers to the hobby. It is suitable for most styles, including the windswept one.

Where to keep them

This species (zone 8) is native to central and southern Asia and is tender in temperate areas. When grown indoors, it needs a bright, sunny, draught-free position and a minimum winter temperature of 12°C (54°F). In summer, move outdoors and place in full sun.

How to look after them

REPOTTING: Repot every 2–3 years, from mid- to late spring. Use free-draining compost consisting of two parts loam, one part peat (or garden compost) and one part sharp sand.

PRUNING AND PINCHING: Sageretias have hard wood, which must be pruned carefully so the bark is not accidentally damaged. In early spring, before the plant

Left: The bark of sageretia peels and flakes as the trunk enlarges, resembling the bark of *Eugenia* (see pages 268–9) and that of plane trees.

starts into growth, remove any damaged or misplaced branches. Regularly prune the new shoots that grow vigorously during the growing season, taking care not to encourage inward growth. Use small, sharp clippers to keep the foliage in shape, as the shoot tips are too stiff for pinching out with fingers. Be careful not to cut through any of the leaves, as this will cause them to discolour and drop.

WIRING: There is rarely any need to wire sageretias because the shaping is achieved through pruning. If branches do need to be wired, it can be applied at any time of the year to hardened shoots. Do not leave the wire in place for longer than a year.

WATERING: Water frequently in summer, but never overwater nor allow the compost to dry out completely. Keep the compost just moist in winter. The leaves will benefit from being misted in summer, especially if plants are kept indoors.

FEEDING: Start feeding sageretias with a general fertilizer in spring, when the new leaves appear. Continue feeding once a month until early autumn.

BE AWARE: Sap-sucking insect pests, such as scale insects, aphids and whitefly, can be a problem. Treat with a systemic insecticide if there are too many to remove by hand. If mildew occurs, water carefully into the compost and improve the humidity around the plant by standing the pot in a tray of pebbles or gravel.

Sageretia thea

Schefflera arboricola

Octopus tree, umbrella tree

- *tender*
- *evergreen*
- *easy to keep*
- *attractive foliage*

This shrub, which in the wild can reach 30m (100ft) high, is familiar to many as a houseplant, when it is more usually about 1m (3ft) high. Its bright green, palmate leaves, composed of 7– 16 leaflets, are borne on slender, flexible stalks. It is tolerant of a range of environments and is one of the easiest indoor bonsai to grow, because it is a true houseplant. The informal upright and clump styles suit this bonsai best. It is also very good for growing on rock. Vast numbers of Schefflera bonsai are produced in Hawaii, but outside the US, this species is not popular for bonsai and not often available.

Where to keep them

The octopus tree (zones 9– 10), which is native to south-east Asia, is tender. It is probably the only indoor bonsai that will tolerate low light levels, and it does best in good but indirect light. Keep out of draughts and make sure that the winter temperature is 16– 20°C (61– 68°F). Octopus tree can be taken outdoors in summer, but there is no need to do this because it is happy indoors all year round.

Left: The foliage of octopus tree is very attractive. The leaves can be washed under a tepid shower occasionally to keep them free of dust.

How to look after them

REPOTTING: Repot every 2– 3 years in early spring. Keeping these plants slightly pot bound restricts leaf size, while frequent repotting will result in large leaves. Use moisture-retentive but free-draining compost consisting of equal parts loam, peat (or garden compost) and sharp sand.

PRUNING AND PINCHING: Cut back branches by half in spring, to encourage the production of dense foliage. During the growing season, maintain the shape of the plant and encourage the growth of secondary shoots by pinching back new shoot tips once two or three leaves have formed.

WIRING: These plants are not wired. The shape of octopus tree bonsai is produced entirely through pruning.

WATERING: Keep the compost just damp at all times, but do not overwater. If grown over lava rock, stand the pot on a tray of gravel so that the roots can grow down into the gravel, from where they will draw up water and nutrients. The leaves will benefit from occasional misting.

FEEDING: Apply a general liquid fertilizer once a month, from spring to late summer.

BE AWARE: Octopus tree is susceptible to scale insects and woolly aphids. If there are too many to remove by hand, apply a weak, systemic insecticide.

Schefflera arboricola

INDOOR/TROPICAL AND SUBTROPICAL BONSAI

Serissa foetida

Serissa, Tree of a thousand stars

- *tender*
- *evergreen*
- *challenging*
- *star-shaped flowers*
- *range of colours*

This small, wiry-stemmed, evergreen shrub has delicate, glossy, dark green leaves, which emit an unpleasant scent (hence *foetida*) when crushed. It produces small, star-shaped, white flowers throughout summer. Variegated forms with cream-edged leaves have been developed, including *Serissa foetida* 'Variegata' and *S.f.* 'Variegated Pink', which has pink flowers. The informal upright and cascade styles are best for this species. Serissa is exported in vast numbers from China for sale as indoor bonsai.

Where to keep them

Serissa (zones 8–10) is a tender plant from south-east Asia, which needs a bright, warm, humid position. If grown indoors, place it on a bright windowsill in summer or, when temperatures are above 22°C (72°F), move it outside into full sun. In winter, when temperatures near the window fall, place in a draught-free area with a temperature of 15–19°C (59–66°F). Although serissa will tolerate short periods at 7°C (45°F), the leaves will drop and branches die back if left in the cold for too long.

Above: The variegated form of serissa has very attractive foliage. A bright environment will encourage colourful leaves.

How to look after them

REPOTTING: Repot, from early to mid-spring, only if the tree is growing strongly; otherwise, it is best to leave your plant well alone, because repotting can do more harm than good. Use a mix of equal parts loam, peat (or garden compost) and sharp sand. Serissa also grows well in peat-based compost with some extra sharp sand added.

PRUNING AND PINCHING: Prune the shoot tips during the growing season to keep the plant in good shape, but be careful not to remove too many of these, because the flowers are borne on the new growth. This plant is not pinched.

WIRING: Serissas take to wiring well, but be careful to wire only the woody branches. Do this between early summer and early autumn, and repeat the process the following year, if necessary. Do not leave the wires on for more than a year.

WATERING: Keep the rootball moist at all times, but allow the compost surface to dry slightly between waterings. Water more frequently in summer than in autumn and winter. Use water that is at room temperature.

FEEDING: Apply a general fertilizer every 2–3 weeks throughout the growing season, but stop feeding for a month in mid-summer. Do not feed immediately after repotting.

BE AWARE: Serissa is a temperamental plant, so do not be discouraged if your first bonsai dies. Scale insects and aphids can be a problem. Spray with an appropriate insecticide at the first sign of infestation.

Serissa foetida 'Variegata'

Tamarindus indica

Tamarind, Indian date

- *tender*
- *evergreen*
- *attractive bark and leaves*
- *difficult as indoor bonsai*

Tamarind is a leguminous tree that originates from Africa but is now spread all over the tropical world. Its botanical name derives from the Arabic *tamar hind*i (Indian date). It is grown extensively in India and south-east Asia for its fruit, while its beautiful, pinnate leaves and wood have many medicinal and other uses. In recent years, tamarind, with its crusty, fissured bark, has become popular for bonsai and it can be trained into any style. It will flower and fruit when fairly young, even when grown as bonsai. It is best sourced from seed or grafted plants.

Where to keep them

Tamarind (zones 9–11) thrives in tropical and subtropical climates, but can be grown as an indoor bonsai in temperate countries if given high humidity and temperature of 10–25°C (50–77°F). Although an evergreen tree, when grown indoors it will lose some of its leaves in winter. Keep in full sun except in the hottest, summer months, when it may need some shade to protect the leaves from burning.

Left: Tamarind bonsai will fruit from quite an early age. This is a bonsai from India.

How to look after them

REPOTTING: Repot every other year, in mid-spring. Use compost consisting of equal parts sand, loam and humus.

PRUNING AND PINCHING: Hard prune in spring. Also, lightly trim and pinch throughout the year. Do not cut off any young flowering shoots.

WIRING: Branches can be wired at any time, and wires left in place for 1–2 years.

WATERING: Although tamarind is drought resistant, never let the soil dry out completely. Nor should you overwater, because it can result in leaf drop and root rot.

FEEDING: Feed in mid-summer, with a low-nitrogen fertilizer, after the flowers have set fruit.

BE AWARE: Tamarind is prone to mildew if kept too wet and if there is insufficient air circulation. Aphids can sometimes be a problem; treat with insecticide.

Tamarindus indica

Triphasia trifolia

Lime berry

- *tender*
- *evergreen*
- *attractive flowers and fruit*
- *difficult as indoor bonsai*

Lime berry is a medicinal plant of the citrus family. It has a distinctive leaves, divided into three leaflets, and white flowers scented like orange blossom. Its fleshy, red fruit is similar to that of *Murraya paniculata* (see pages 286–7). A native of south-east Asia, this plant is a relative newcomer to the bonsai world, but is now used quite extensively in Indonesia and many south-east Asian countries. It is best treated as a tropical bonsai, but with perserverance it may survive as an indoor one in temperate climates. Lime berry is easy to germinate from seed, and it makes a good bonsai in a relatively short time.

Above: The crimson-coloured fruit of the lime berry resemble miniature oranges, but of a different hue.

Where to keep them

Lime berry (zones 9–11) is easy to grow as outdoor bonsai in the tropics in full sun or partial shade. As an indoor bonsai in temperate climates it needs as much light as possible, as well as a minimum temperature of 10°C (50°F).

How to look after them

REPOTTING: Repot every 2–3 years, in spring, using compost consisting of equal parts sand and loam.

PRUNING AND PINCHING: Regular pruning will keep the tree dense and twiggy.

WIRING: There is no real need to wire.

WATERING: Keep soil moist year-round, but not soaking wet.

FEEDING: Feed with a high-nitrogen fertilizer in the early part of the year and use a low-nitrogen feed when fruit appears.

BE AWARE: Lime berry is prone to greenhouse pests, such as aphids and red spider mites; treat with insecticides.

Triphasia trifolia

Ulmus parvifolia
Chinese elm

- *hardy*
- *deciduous or semi-evergreen*
- *easy to keep*
- *versatile*

This is undoubtedly the best 'starter' bonsai for beginners, because it is easy to grow, reliable and suitable for any bonsai style. Millions are exported from China every year in all shapes, styles and sizes. Chinese elm is sometimes sold as 'Zelkova' or *Zelkova sinensis* to get around import regulations, but these are not true *Zelkova* (see pages 168–9). Chinese elm for indoor bonsai should not be confused with the hardier forms, which have a rough bark (see pages 166–7). Plants that are grown indoors all year round will be semi-evergreen (or even evergreen), while outdoor specimens will lose their leaves in winter.

Where to keep them

Indoor Chinese elm bonsai (zones 6–9) likes lots of light, so keep it in a bright position, such as a windowsill. It does better in a cool (10°C/50°F) room than a warm one. Chinese elm bonsai can also be grown outdoors, because it tolerates wide temperature variations.

How to look after them

REPOTTING: Repot Chinese elm only when pot bound. This is best done in early spring, as the new leaves are about to emerge. Most commercial bonsai can be left in the original pot for at least two

Left: The serrated leaves of Chinese elm are mid- to dark green in colour. In autumn, they turn yellow/orange and may be shed.

years from the time of purchase. Use Akadama soil or peat-based compost consisting of two parts peat (or garden compost) and one part sharp sand.

PRUNING AND PINCHING: In early spring, prune out any unwanted branches. Thin out the fine branches, as necessary. Keep the plant looking neat by pinching out new shoot tips, as soon as two or three leaves have emerged on the stem.

WIRING: Most shaping is achieved through pruning. If you do need to wire Chinese elm, do so between late spring and mid-autumn. The wires can be left on for a year.

WATERING: Keep the compost moist at all times, but do not overwater. It is better to wait until the surface of the compost has dried out a little between waterings. Plants need less water in winter than in summer. Chinese elm prefers fairly humid conditions, so stand the bonsai pot in a shallow tray filled with pebbles or gravel. Misting the plants occasionally will also be beneficial.

FEEDING: Feed with a general fertilizer between spring and autumn, when the plant is growing.

BE AWARE: When it is grown indoors, Chinese elm is very susceptible to red spider mites, aphids and whitefly. Sudden loss of leaves is usually a sign of infestation, so spray with an appropriate insecticide. Standing the tree outside and spraying with a jet of water will dislodge many insects. Indoor Chinese elm is prone to die-back if the twigs become too congested, so thin branches. Its foliage sometimes turns yellow and drops; this is often caused by a change in the plant's environment.

Ulmus parvifolia

Zanthoxylum piperitum

Japan pepper

- *hardy*
- *deciduous*
- *easy to keep*
- *attractive foliage*
- *red berries*

This tree is the source of Sichuan peppercorns. It has glossy, dark green, pinnate leaves, which turn yellow in autumn. In early summer, greenish-yellow flowers appear, and these are followed by tiny, red berries. The bark is aromatic. Japan pepper is an attractive subject for indoor bonsai. Although it was introduced only recently from China to the outside world as a bonsai, it was already popular as an easy-to-keep indoor subject. This plant is best grown in the informal upright style.

Above: The small, glossy, pinnate leaves of Japan pepper are both attractive and highly aromatic, as is the bark.

Where to keep them

Japan pepper (zones 7– 10) originates from China, Korea, Japan and Taiwan. It is hardy in temperate areas, although as a bonsai it should be treated as an indoor plant. Keep it in a bright position, such as on a windowsill, but move it outdoors during summer and stand it in full sun.

How to look after them

REPOTTING: Repot Japan peppers every other year. The best time to do this is in mid-spring, just before the new leaves emerge. Use free-draining, loam-based compost.

PRUNING AND PINCHING: Hard pruning is necessary only if you wish to restructure the branches. During the growing season, keep the tree looking trim by cutting back new growth and pinching out the growing tips when two to three sets of compound leaves have sprouted.

WIRING: Japan pepper has very stiff branches that are not suitable for conventional wiring. Hold the branches in place with guy wires (see page 33). Leave these on for at least a year, while the branches set.

WATERING: Make sure that Japan pepper is well watered throughout the growing season. In winter, keep the compost just moist. If the compost is allowed to dry out completely, the plant will die. Misting is advisable if the room's atmosphere is very dry.

FEEDING: Apply a high-nitrogen fertilizer in spring, when the plant starts into growth. From summer until autumn, give a general fertilizer once a month.

BE AWARE: Aphids will cluster on new shoots. If the plant is standing outside, remove them by jetting them with water. Otherwise, pick them off by hand or apply an appropriate systemic insecticide.

Zanthoxylum piperitum

Index

Page numbers in *italics* refer
to illustration captions.

A

Acacia 242–3
  A. burkei 242
  A. dealbata 242
  A. galpinii 242
  A. howittii 243
  A. nigrescens 242
  A. paradoxa 242
  A. podalyriifolia 243
Acer 21, 23, 32, 38, 45, *107*, 232
  A. buergerianum 107, 108–9,
    110
  A. campestre 110–11
  A. palmatum 107, 112–13, 115,
    116, 146
  A. p. 'Aka Shigitatsu-sawa' 116
  A. p. 'Arakawa' 116
  A. p. 'Asahi-zuru' 116
  A. p. 'Beni-chidori' 114
  A. p. 'Deshōjō' 114, 115
  A. p. 'Higasayama' 116
  A. p. 'Kashima-yatsubusa'
    116–17
  A. p. 'Kiyohime' *116*, 117
  A. p. 'Koto-no-ito' 117
  A. p. 'Kurui-jishi' 117
  A. p. 'Mikawa-yatsubusa' 117
  A. p. 'Seigai' 114–15
  A. p. 'Shishio' 114, 115
  A. p. var. *dissectum* 'Seiryu' 117
  A. p. var. *d.* 'Shigitatsu-sawa' 117
  A. p. var. *d.* 'Shishigashira' 117
  A. p. var. *d.* 'Ukon' 117
Adansonia digitata 244–5
adelgids 40
Adenium 246–7
  A. obesum 246

Aesculus hippocastanum 107,
    118–19
age 19
Akadama 36
alder 120–1
  black 120
  common 120
  Italian 120
Alnus 120–1
  A. cordata 120
  A. glutinosa 120, *121*
aphids 40
apricot 212
  Japanese 212, 214
ash 23, 136–7
  common 136
  manna 136
  white 136
azalea, satsuki *7, 19,173*,
    222–3

B

bamboo, Buddha's belly 241
  heavenly 241
Bambusa ventricosa 241
banyan 272
  Chinese 270
baobab 244–5
barberry 174–5
Beaucarnea 241
beech 23, 38, *39*, 45, 134–5
  Antarctic 150–1
  common 134
  Japanese white 134
Berberis 174–5
  B. darwinii 174
  B. thunbergii 174, *175*
Betula 122–3
  B. pendula 122, *123*
  B. utilis 122

birch 122–3
  Himalayan 122
  silver 122
blackthorn 212, 214–15
bleaching 33
bo tree 273
bonsai 6–7, 10
  21 styles 10–11
  bonsai care 14
  bonsai today 13
  broad-leaved species 106–7
  China 11–12
  compost 36
  conifers 44–5
  exhibitions and competitions 15
  first steps 15
  flowering bonsai 172–3
  Japan 12
  pricing bonsai 18–19
  problems 40–1
  propagation 20, 38–9
  repotting 37
  selecting plant 17
  space requirements 15
  temperature and light 36
  where to buy 16–17
bottlebrush 252–3
  crimson 252
  weeping 252
Bougainvillea 20, *241*, 248–9
  B. glabra 248
  B. spectabilis 248
  B. x buttiana 248
box 124–5
  Chinese 286–7
boxwood 124–5
broad-leaved species 106–7
broom style 156, 166, 168, 264
buckeye 118–19
bush clover, Japanese 202–3

buttonwood 132–3
Buxus 124–5
 B. harlandii 124
 B. sempervirens 125

C
Calliandra 250–1
 C. haematocephala 250
Callistemon 252–3
 C. citrinus 252, *253*
 C. viminalis 252
Camellia 173, 176–7, 228
 C. japonica 177
Carmona microphylla 241, 254–5
Carpinus 39, 107
 C. betulus 126–7, 128
 C. laxiflora 128–9
 C. turczaninowii 130–1
cascade style 64, 78, 86, 88, 196,
  200, 210, 278
Cassia 241
Casuarina 256–7
 C. equisetifolia 256, *257*
cedar 46–7
 Atlas 46
 Cyprus 46
 eastern white 100–1
 Japanese 38, 44, 52–3
 of Lebanon 46
Cedrus 44, 46–7
 C. atlantica 46, *47*
 C. a. Glauca Group 46
 C. brevifolia 46
 C. deodara 46
 C. libani 46
Celtis sinensis 258–9
Chaenomeles japonica 173, 178–9,
  218
Chamaecyparis 39, 44, 48–9
 C. obtusa 38, 48–9, 100–1
 C. pisifera 48, *49*, 50–1, *51*
 C. p. 'Boulevard' 50
 C. p. 'Plumosa' 50
cherry 38, 212–13
 Asiatic cornelian 180

bird plum 300–1
 Brazilian 268
 cornelian 180
 downy 212, 216–17
 Fuji 212
 Nanking 212, 216–17
 oriental 212
 Surinam 268
 Yoshino 212
chestnut, horse 118–19
cinquefoil 210–11
Citrus 260–1
climate zones 22–3
 Mediterranean zone 23–4
 plant hardiness zones 25
 temperate zone 23
 tropical zone 24
clubs 15
clump style 178, 182, 302
competitions 15
compost 36
conifers 44
 care of conifers 44–5
 deciduous 44
 evergreen 44
 popular conifers for bonsai 45
Conocarpus erectus 132–3
cornel 180–1
Cornus 180–1
 C. mas 180, *181*
 C. officinalis 180
Corylopsis spicata 182–3
cotoneaster 184–5, 220
 herringbone 184
Cotoneaster 184–5, 220
 C. horizontalis 184, *185*
 C. integrifolius 184
crab apple 39, *173*, 204–5
 Hall's 204
 Japanese 204
 Kaido 204
 Makino 204
 Siberian 204
Crassula 262–3
 C. arborescens 262

 C. ovata 262, *263*
Crataegus 21, 173
 C. laevigata 186–7
 C. monogyna 186, 188–9
Cryptomeria japonica 38, 44, 52–3
Cuphea hyssopifolia 264–5
cuttings 38–9
Cycas 241
cypress 39, 44, 48–9
 bald 96–7
 deciduous 96–7
 Hinoki 38, 48–9
 Sawara 48, 50–1
 swamp 96–7

D
date, Indian 306–7
deodar 46
desert rose 246–7
diseases 41
dogwood 180–1
dollar plant 262
driftwood style 10, *12*, *19*, 33, 54,
  58, 59, 62, 66, 78, 88, 98,
  112, 114, 124, 132, 144,
  148, 204, 248, 288, 296
Duranta erecta 266–7

E
Elaeagnus 173, 190–1
 E. multiflora 190
 E. pungens 190, *191*
elm 23, 38, 164–5
 American 164
 Chinese *11*, 166–7, 310–11
 Florida 164
 Japanese grey-bark 168–9
 slippery 164
 Texas cedar 164
 white 164
Eucalyptus 23
Eugenia 268–9, 300
 E. brasiliensis 268
 E. uniflora 268, *269*
Euphorbia pulcherrima 241

exhibitions 15
ezo matsu 76–7

F
Fagus 23, 38, 39, 45, 107, 134–5
    F. crenata 134
    F. sylvatica 134
feeding 35
Ficus 21, 241, 270–1
    F. aurea 272
    F. benghalensis 272
    F. benjamina 270
    F. b. var. nuda 272
    F. boxifolia 273
    F. burt-davii 'Nana' 273
    F. carica 192–3
•   F. infectoria 273
    F. microcarpa 240, 270
    F. m. 'Green Island' 21, 271
    F. m. 'Long Island' 273
    F. natalensis 272
    F. nerifolia 270
    F. pelkan 272
    F. religiosa 273
    F. rubiginosa 273
    F. rumphii 273
    F. salicifolia 273
    F. tomentosa 272
    F. virens 272
fig 21, 270–1
    box-leaved 273
    common 192–3
    edible 192–3
    Florida 272
    Port Jackson 273
    strangler 272
    veld 273
    weeping 270
fireblight 41
firethorn 220–1
flat-top style 242
flowering bonsai 172–3
forest plantings 72, 128, 136, 204
formal upright style 48, 74, 118,
    218, 258

Forsythia 194–5
    F. suspensa 194
    F. x intermedia 194, 195
Fortune, Robert 182
Fortunella 241
    F. hindsii 260, 261
Fraxinus 23, 136–7
    F. americana 136
    F. excelsior 136, 137
    F. orna 136
fringe flower, Chinese 284–5
Fuchsia 13, 274–5
    F. reflexa 275
fuji 236
Fukien tea 254–5

G
galls 41
Gardenia jasminoides 276–7
gardenia, common 276–7
geography 22
Ginkgo biloba 138–9
golden bell 194
golden dewdrop 266–7
goumi 190
goyo matsu 80–1
grapevine 234–5
group plantings 72, 128
gum 23

H
hackberry, Chinese 258–9
    Japanese 258–9
Hamamelis 284
hawthorn 21
    common hedging 188–9
    Midland 186–7
    red 186–7
heather, false 264–5
Hedera 140–1
    H. helix 141
hemlock 102–3
    eastern 102
    northern Japanese 44, 102
    southern Japanese 102

western 102
Hibiscus 241
hime ringo 204–5
holidays 7, 14, 21
hollow-trunk effects 33, 130,
    248, 249
holly, box-leaved 278–9
    common 142–3
    Japanese 198–9, 278–9
honeysuckle, hedging 107,
    148–9
hornbeam 39
    common 126–7
    Japanese 128–9
    Korean 130–1
horsetail tree 256
Hydrangea anomala subsp.
    petiolaris 196–7
hydrangea, climbing 196

I
ichi 98–9
icho 138–9
Ilex aquifolium 142–3
    I. crenata 278–9
    I. serrata 198–9
indoor bonsai 18, 21, 240–1
    environment for 25
    watering 35
informal style 182, 184, 198,
    200, 228
informal upright style 74, 78, 80,
    86, 88, 118, 144, 156, 166,
    176, 190, 196, 206, 210, 218,
    222, 254, 258, 268, 276, 278,
    282, 298, 302, 312
ivy 140–1
    Boston 154
Ixora 241

J
Jacaranda 241
jade plant 262
    silver 262
jasmine, Cape 276–7

orange 286–7
winter 200–1
Jasminum nudiflorum 200–1
jins 33, 58, 98
Juglans 23
juniper 23, 36, 38, 44, 48
  California 54–5
  Chinese 19, 56–7
  needle 18, 66–7
  procumbens 64–5
  Sabina 68–9
  Shimpaku 54, 58, 296
  squamata 70–1
  temple 66–7
Juniperus 23, 36, 38, 44, 48, 164
  J. californica 54–5
  J. chinensis 19, 45, 56–7, 68
  J. c. 'Blaauw' 60
  J. c. 'Globosa Cinerea' 59
  J. c. 'Itoigawa' 54, 57, 58–9
  J. c. 'Kaizuka' 61
  J. c. 'Kishu' 59, 60
  J. c. 'Shimpaku' 54, 58, 296
  J. c. 'Tohoku' 59
  J. c. var. *sargentii* 59
  J. communis 45, 62–3
  J. c. 'Hornibrookii' 62
  J. c. 'Repanda' 62
  J. procumbens 21, 45, 64–5
  J. p. 'Nana' 65
  J. rigida 19, 45, 66–7
  J. sabina 68–9
  J. squamata 45, 70–1
  J. s. 'Meyeri' 70
  J. x pfitzeriana 68

K
kaede 108–9
kangaroo thorn 242
kara matsu 72–3
Kimura, Masahiko 33
knob thorn 242
kumquat, dwarf 260
kuro matsu 88–9
kusamaki 294

L
Lagerstroemia indica 280–1
landscape style 11
Lantana 241
larch 23, 38, 44, 72–3
  American 72
  Chinese 90–1
  European 72
  false 90–1
  golden 90–1
  Japanese 72
Larix 23, 38, 44, 72–3
  L. decidua 72, 73, 90
  L. kaempferi 72, 90
  L. laricina 72
laurel, Indian 270
layering 39
lemon trees 260 1
lentisc 290–1
Lespedeza bicolor 202–3
light 36
Ligustrum 282–3
  L. lucidum 282–3
  L. sinense 282–3
  L. vulgare 144–5, 282
lime 162–3
lime berry 308–9
linden 162–3
liquid amber 146–7
Liquidambar styraciflua 146–7
literati style 86, 136, 162, 204,
  210, 212
Lonicera nitida 106, 148–9
Loropetalum chinense 284–5
  L. c. var. *rubrum* 284

M
maidenhair tree 138–9
Malus 39, 173, 204–5
  M. baccata 204, *205*
  M. floribunda 204
  M. halliana 204
  M. x micromalus 204
mame 18, 200, 262
maple 21, 23, 32, 38, 45

field 110–11
  hedge 110–11
  Japanese 13, 112–13
  mountain 112–13
  three-toothed 108–9
  trident 10, 11, 108–9
mastic tree 290–1
Mediterranean zone 23–4
Metasequoia glyptostroboides
  44, 74–5
mildew 41
mimosa 242
monkey thorn 242
  black 242
mophead style 264
Morus 206–7
  M. alba 206
  M. nigra 206
  M. rubra 206
  M. r. 'Nana' *207*
mulberry 206–7
  black 206
  red 206
  white 206
multi-trunk style 128
Murraya paniculata 286–7, 308
myrtle, common 208–9
  crepe 280–1
Myrtus 241
  M. communis 208–9

N
Nandina domestica 241
natsu-tsubaki 228
natural tree style 118
Nolina 241
Nothofagus antarctica 150–1

O
oak 23
  common 156–7
  cork 158–9
  English 156–7
  she 256–7
octopus tree 302–3

Olea 23
  O. sylvestris 152–3
olive 23, 152–3
  thorny 190
orange trees 260–1
outdoor bonsai 18, 20–1
  watering 34–5

P
palm, sago 241
Parthenocissus 154–5
  P. quinquefolia 154
  P. tricuspidata 154
peach 212
peach leaf curl 41
pemphis 288–9
Pemphis acidula 288–9
pepper, Japan 312–13
pests 40–1
Picea 23, 44
  P. abies 76
  P. jezoensis 19, 76–7
Pierneef style 242
pinching 14, 30
pine 21, 23, 33, 36, 38, 44
  Buddhist 294
  blackjack 82–3
  cork-bark Japanese black 88
  dwarf mountain 45, 78–9
  Japanese black 88–9
  Japanese five needle 80–1
  Japanese white 80–1
  Monterey 84–5
  Ponderosa
  Scots 86–7
  Swiss mountain 45, 78–9
  Western yellow 82–3
Pinus 21, 23, 33, 36, 38, 44, 72
  P. mugo 45, 78–9
  P. parviflora 45, 48, 80–1
  P. p. 'Kokonoe' 80
  P. p. 'Zui-sho' 80
  P. ponderosa 82–3
  P. radiata 84–5
  P. sylvestris 45, 86–7

P. s. 'Beuvronensis' 86
P. thunbergii 45, 80, 88–9, 256
P. t. var. *corticosa* 88
Pistacia lentiscus 290–1
pitanga 268
Pithecellobium tortum 292–3
plant hardiness zones 25
plant needs 22
plant selection 17
  good-quality plants 17
  matching plant to setting 17
  optimum characteristics 17–18
  season of purchase 18
  species 19
  type of tree 18
plum, cherry 212
Podocarpus 21, 294–5
  P. macrophyllus 294
  P. nivalis 294, 295
poinsettia 241
pomegranate 298–9
Potentilla 173
  P. fruticosa 210–11
powder-puff tree 250-1
Premna 296–7
  P. microphylla 296, 297
  P. serratifolia 296
privet 282–3
  Chinese 282–3
  common 144–5
problems 40
  diseases 41
  excessive leaf drop 40
  pests 40–1
  yellowing leaves 40
propagation 20, 38
  cuttings 38–9
  layering 39
  pros and cons 39
  seeds 38
pruning 14, 20, 28–30
  leaf pruning 30
  pruning branches 29
Prunus 38, 173, 212–13
  P. armeniaca 212

P. cerasifera 212
P. incisa 212, *213*
P. mume 212, 214
P. persica 212
P. serrulata 212
P. spinosa 212, 214–15
P. tomentosa 212, 216–17
P. x subhirtella 'Autumnalis'
  212
P. x yedoensis 212
Pseudocydonia sinensis 173,
  218–19
Pseudolarix amabilis 90–1
Punica granatum 298–9
  P. g. var. *nana* 298
Pyracantha angustifolia 172, 173,
  220–1

Q
Quercus 23
  Q. robur 107, 156–7
  Q. suber 106, 158–9
quince, Chinese 218–19
  flowering 178–9

R
rain tree, Brazilian 292–3
red spider mites 40
redwood, California 94–5
  coastal 92–3
  dawn 74–5
  giant 94–5
repotting 37
  how to repot 37
  time of year 37
reshaping 20
Rhododendron indicum 19, 173,
  222–3
  R. simsii 222
root-over-rock style *106, 108, 112,*
  172, 184, 302
Rosa 224–5
rosemary 226–7
roses 224–5
Rosmarinus officinalis 226–7

S

Sagaretia thea 300–1
Salix 39, 107
  S. babyonica 160–1
satin wood 286–7
savin 68–9
scale insects 40
Schefflera arboricola 302–3
seeds 38
Sequoia sempervirens 92–3
Sequoiadendron giganteum 94–5
Serissa foetida 241, 296, 304–5
  S. f. 'Variegata' 304, 305
  S. f. 'Variegated Pink' 304
sharis 33, 58, 98
shohin 18, 200
silverthorn 190
size 19
slanting style 86
sloe 212, 214–15
snowbell, Japanese 230–1
space requirements 15
spruce 23, 44
  Norway 76
  yezo 19, 76–7
Stewartia 173, 228–9
  S. monadelpha 228, 229
  S. pseudocamellia 228
stewartia, Japanese 7, 228
structural shaping 28
stuartia 228–9
Styrax 173
  S. japonicus 230–1
sugi 52–3
sweet gum 146–7

T

tamarind 306–7
Tamarindus indica 306–7
tamarisk 39
Tamarix 39
Taxodium distichum 96–7
Taxus 98–9
  T. baccata 98–9
  T. cuspidata 98, 99

temperate zone 23
temperature 36
thorn tree 242–3
Thuja occidentalis 100–1
Tilia 162–3
  T. cordata 162
tools 28, 33
  power tools 33, 130, 152
tosho 66–7
totara, Alpine 294
tree of a thousand stars 304–5
Triphasia trifolia 308–9
tropical zone 24
Tsuga 102–3
  T. canadensis 102
  T. diversifolia 102, 103
  T. heterophylla 102
  T. sieboldii 102
twin trunk style 128

U

Ulmus 23, 38, 107, 164–5, 168, 258
  U. americana 164
  U. a. var. floridana 164, 165
  U. crassifolia 164
  U. parvifolia 164, 166–7, 241,
    310–11
  U. p. 'Catlin' 164
  U. p. 'Hokkaido' 164
  U. p. 'Nire' 164
  U. p. 'Uzen' 164
  U. rubra 164, 165
umbrella tree 302–3

V

Viburnum 232–3
  V. lantana 233
vine weevils 40–1
Virginia creeper 154–5
Vitis vinifera 234–5

W

walnut 23
watering 14, 21, 34
  broad-leaved species 106

conifers 45
  indoor bonsai 35
  outdoor bonsai 34–5
wattle 242–3
  Queensland silver 243
weeping style 160, 243
wellingtonia 94–5
willow 39
  weeping 160–1
windswept style 78, 86, 112, 114,
    158, 162, 204, 212, 286, 300
winterberry, Japanese 198–9
wiring 20, 31
  guy wires 33
  how to wire 32
  wire type and size 31–2
wisteria 173, 236–7
  Chinese 236
  Japanese 236
Wisteria 236–7
  W. floribunda 236
  W. f. 'Kuchi-beni' 237
  W. sinensis 236
witch hazel 284
  Japanese 182–3

Y

yamamomiji 112–13
yew 98–8
  Chinese 294
  common 98–9
  English 98–9
  Japanese 98–9

Z

Zanthoxylum piperitum 312–13
Zelkova 310
  Z. serrata 168–9
  Z. sinensis 310
Zen Buddhism 6, 12

Acknowledgements

Picture credits

All photographs are courtesy Peter Chan, with the exception of the following.

Alamy Andy Sween 84; Bob Gibbons 54; Heather Angel/Natural Visions 96; Paul Sterry/Nature Photographers 94; Brian Gladsby/Science Photo Library 212

Ausbonsai.com.au 253

Australian National Bonsai Collection Leigh Taafe 243, 253

Dan Barton 205

Bonsai Focus The International Bonsai Magazine/Bonsaifocus.com 296

Mike Bush 288

Charles Ceronio 242

Jonas Dupuich/BonsaiTonight.com 51, 54, 55, 65, 83, 85, 92, 93, 95, 125, 147, 193, 281

Flickr tanakawho 202

Fotolia M Schuppich 100

Garden World Images Nathalie Pasquel/MAP 124; Nicole et Patrick Mioulane/MAP 309

Rob Kempinski 101,165

Steve Moore 82

Jim Osborne 123

D Ravindran 245, 307

Shutterstock Walter Pall 215

Robert Steven 257, 289, 297, 309

Leigh Taafe/Australian National Bonsai Collection 243, 253

Thinkstock Crosbygrisu 154

Wikipedia The Botanist 308

Author thanks

I would like to thank my many bonsai friends in the UK, USA, India, Indonesia, Australia, South Africa and Brazil for letting me photograph their trees. I would also like to thank those who generously contributed pictures for species that we cannot grow in the United Kingdom.

All the best,

Peter